SPIRITUAL HEALTH AND HEALING

SPIRITUAL HEALTH AND HEALING

BY

HORATIO W. DRESSER, Ph.D.

Author of "The Power of Silence," "A History of the New Thought Movement," "The Open Vision," etc.

GYAN

Published by

Gyan Publishing House
5, Ansari Road
Daryaganj, New Delhi-110002
Phone: 011-47034999, 9811692060
E-mail: books@gyanbooks.com

Distribution Network
gyanbooks.com
India, USA, Canada, UK, Australia, France

ISBN : 978-81-212-6298-9 (PB)
First Published, 1922

2nd Impression 2022

Printed at: Gyan Press, Delhi.

SPIRITUAL HEALTH AND HEALING
Author: HORATIO W. DRESSER, Ph.D.

SPIRITUAL HEALTH AND HEALING

BY

HORATIO W. DRESSER, Ph.D.

Author of "The Power of Silence," "A History of the New Thought Movement," "The Open Vision," etc.

PREFACE

INTEREST in spiritual healing has reached a point where it is no longer necessary to dwell on such elementary matters as the influence of fear and worry, the power of suggestion and the utilizing of the subconscious. These considerations are now taken for granted by those who believe that inner healing is more than mental. Suggestion is not regarded as decisive except by those who would ignore the spiritual life and limit healing to the sphere of psychology. For those of us who believe that the spiritual life is inseparable from true spiritual healing, the question of mental influences and mental methods is forever secondary. It ought rather to be a question of cultivating the mode of life which produces spiritual health. All our efforts should be constructive. Our clues should be drawn from the ideal, not through study of conditions which produce disease.

To be normal, to live in spiritual health is to be in accord with the universe: to think, will, live by the Divine order. Spiritual health is the standard set for man by God's purpose in bringing him into being. It is man's birthright as heir of the heavenly kingdom. It is inherent in his nature as created in the Divine image and likeness. Jesus came among us to disclose that standard in its fulness, and establish it in the minds and hearts of men by inspiring works and words. He promised greater works when it should become a social ideal. He taught that wisdom which should become man's guide in living the life which produces health and freedom. A spiritual science was implied in those teachings. A spiritual art was exemplified by those works and words of healing. Those who would be true followers ought to give this science first place, taking the clue from Christ as archetype.

Interest in spiritual health begins from above and works down, from within and works out. Ordinary healing is from below and is concerned with measures of relief and the improvement of man's material environment. Christ bids man so live that health shall always radiate from him as virtue radiates from one whose religion is "to do good." Thus health is made a secondary consideration in comparison with that larger, more splendid life which manifests health as one of the signs of its beauty. Health is to be a result of the abundant life. It will come as a consequence, just as our tastes change, our manners become more gentle, our affections more constant, our faces more radiant through the inner touch of the Spirit.

In the following pages this philosophy of the Christ is taken for granted. Many writers have taught it in their favorite ways, since the time of P. P. Quimby, who was the first healer in our day to plead for a "Science of the Christ." This philosophy includes the idea of the Divine indwelling as the guiding principle of the inner life, of the spiritual world as the nearby source of real power; the idea that there is a heavenly purpose in our strivings, that the natural world is a theatre for the development of the soul. If different writers would express these introductory matters in various ways, all would agree that the endeavor to live by this higher wisdom is the great consideration.

The chief need at present is for a clearer statement of the ideas which lead beyond mental to spiritual healing. Some teachers would put the whole matter in the present tense, affirming the ideal as realized now, making light of the natural world with its opportunities, and passing by the ages of philosophic thought. Hence they would identify man in his real selfhood with "the Christ within" and end the matter with ever-varying affirmations turning upon one idea. Others would maintain that we make no headway except through acknowledgment of "the light of Christ in the soul" as leading us on to greater and greater attainments. While they would agree that man in spirit already exists in the Divine image and likeness, they would find reality and meaning in his progress from stage to stage in the natural world. It would seem clear that the truth of the Christ is too great and too wonderful to be apprehended except as man looks up to the Master, admitting that he has more and more to learn. It is this view which we plead for. A new statement of this ideal is called for because the trend of thought among people interested in inner healing is too much the other way. We hope to show that this philosophy of upliftment toward the Christ is the true view of spiritual healing.

A word seems to be called for concerning "A History of the New Thought Movement," 1919. Some reviewers have complained because I did not indulge in adverse criticisms. But I had supposed a historian should be impartial. I was telling a story, not commenting on its reality or truth. In other volumes, especially "A Handbook of the New Thought," 1917, I had made critical estimates enough; pointing out that the psychology of the New Thought is one-sided, that some leaders tend to exalt the human self so as to make it a god, thereby advocating egotism instead of spiritual healing. My interest in the movement was to call attention afresh to its beginnings, in order to emphasize the fact that the therapeutic movement had not realized its spiritual standard. Since 1919, the remaining branches of the movement, save one, have been united in an effort to make the Christ the cardinal principle. It is now a question of looking forward to see what the movement will make of the Christ as its ideal.

Critics of New Thought and Christian Science in its various forms have pointed out that we are not "parts" of God, because God is one and indivisible; that man is not "life in itself," for God only is *life in itself;* that man is not "one with God," but may be conjoined with Him through responsiveness: hence that man's recipiency of life is measured by his *love,* not by his affirmation or thought. These discriminations point the way beyond mysticism and pantheism in all its forms, beyond self-centredness and mere thought to the ideal of constancy of love for God and man in frank recognition of our sonship. The whole outlook changes with the adoption of this higher point of view. We realize that the spiritual life has hardly begun, since it is rather a gift of the Spirit in us than the work of our efforts at self-control and efficiency in the use of thought. It changes too because we adopt the idea of a spiritual incoming of power, touching the inmost being first, then quickening the understanding, spreading through mental life as a whole. The ideal is no longer a mere settling down into self in poise and composure, as if we had nothing to acknowledge and nothing to overcome; it is the attainment of inner openness to the Spirit, that the Divine life may freely course through all channels. It means that regeneration is still essential, hence that we need to make ready by purifying our desires, living on simpler food, keeping closer to nature, and avoiding anything like drugs and stimulants which clog and impede. Right thinking assumes its proper place at last as instrumental to right living. The life is a test in a far deeper way than we had realized. There is something better than being either healed or cured. We need a nobler prevailing love. We need practical Christianity in all its fulness. We need the inner or spiritual Word. We need the living Christ, the glorified Lord. This is the great truth of the New Age. Interest in spiritual healing is one of the tendencies of life today which point to this truth. We have not begun to interpret it aright until we regard the healing movement in this its relation to the new time. We may therefore pass beyond the crudities and extravagant claims in quest of the really spiritual element. The discerning reader will find in these pages a very different way of stating the whole matter, and will proceed to test it by direct reference to life, in contrast with the mere criticism of theories.

The best way, in fact, to overcome the limitations of those who have not grasped the full idea of spiritual healing is to look back to the prophetic teachings of the New Age. For some this will mean deeper study of the writings of Swedenborg. For others it will mean profounder knowledge of Dr. Quimby's philosophy. In writing this volume I have had both of these interests in mind. Some of the chapters are concerned with Swedenborg's theory of the Divine influx. In others I have tried to make a clearer statement of the ideas and methods which Dr. Quimby sets forth in his manuscripts. This book may then be regarded as an estimate of the Quimby method of healing. It is not written in Quimby's terms. I have not assumed that Quimby's view is in every way superior to ideas now passing current. But it was the original view, it contained the spiritual impetus which gave rise to the modern therapeutic movement, it was the result of many years of pioneer work in this field, and it is still the view by which we may most directly test our own ideas and methods. My parents were patients under Quimby's care in Portland, Maine, and from Dr. Quimby they learned the method of silent healing which is here advocated. I have felt it a duty I owed to humanity both to publish the manuscripts and to make my own statement of the ideas and methods which have come down to us from Quimby. I began to put this work in final form with the publication of "The Power of Silence," Boston, 1895. The present volume completes this work, as the prime result of a later study of Quimby's writings.

CONTENTS

CONTENTS

SPIRITUAL HEALTH AND HEALING

I

THE POWER OF THE SPIRIT

Two generations ago, in a small New England city, a promising young man of twenty-two lay apparently at the point of death. On both sides of his house the ancestors were physically weak, and all save two in a family of nine had already passed from this life when our record begins. The young man of whom we are speaking was frail in physique. There seemed to be little power of resistance to withstand the oncoming of a disease ordinarily accounted fatal as matters go in this world of allegiance to material things. In type he was spiritually minded and highly intuitive, inclined to think for himself and exercise rights of individual initiative. He was zealous in religion, devoted to the church, eager in fact to prepare himself for the ministry if his health should permit the completion of his college course. On the side of faith as conventionally understood nothing more could indeed have been asked.

He had joined the church at sixteen with a large measure of emotional enthusiasm. He regularly attended all services and was especially zealous in prayer-meeting. He was a Calvinist, however, in the thorough-going sense of the word. God to him was little more than a Man seated on a white throne of authority outside the world, a God to be admired with awesome reverence rather than a Father to be loved. Naturally our young man, devout as he was, had no idea of the power of divine love as an indwelling presence to be sought as one might turn to a friend. Christianity was a doctrine of salvation interpreted as a Baptist of the period understood it. Salvation as thus conceived by no means included the problems of bodily weakness and ill-health. Prayer was for certain purposes. The observances decreed by the church were to be rigidly adhered to, leaving mundane matters for consideration in their proper place. Among these matters was the question of disease, and the physicians of the old school had apparently done their utmost to save this young man.

Then there came from a wholly unexpected source a marvellous change into this young life. This change not only meant that he was rescued from the abyss of death by spiritual means when material methods had failed, but that he was given a new impetus and an understanding of life which enabled him to live on this earth during many years of great usefulness. It will be worth while considering what wrought the change, why it could be so pronounced in the case of a man emphatically spiritual in type, genuinely a Christian as the Gospel was then understood.

There came as if heaven-sent a man whose work among the sick had no place among therapeutic systems commonly known as scientific. He did not give medicines or drugs. He had no system of physical treatment. Nor did he even diagnose disease by its symptoms, or inquire into verdicts pronounced by those competent to make a diagnosis. He received as patients those whose faith gave them impetus enough to visit his office or send for him. Without asking questions, he sat meditatively by his patients to gather whatever impressions might come intuitively by his own way of seeking such discernment. Having gained his impression and sought light on the problem before him, he put his mind through a realization akin to prayer as an act of worship, but more effective than such prayers as our young man was wont to hear on Friday evenings at church. He believed that

God is directly accessible through prayer, yet with additional faith in the immediate response of the human spirit as potential master of the body. This definite and practical faith implied the utilizing of healing power to restore the body through the spirit. Proceeding by his own method, he ventured to seek help from within when all hope of a cure through conventional methods had passed. For in his practice with the sick he was not governed by outward appearances or even by signs which indicate the near-by presence of death. What signified was the state of a person's spirit and the possibility of leading a responsive person into the light out of the darkness of threatening miseries and fears.

Many people were restored to health by this true believer in the presence of God, some of whom became active workers when they grasped the principle. The world has since become familiar with the idea of mental healing, and is quick to arrive at the conclusion that this is what one means, namely, that by the influence of one mind on another through "suggestion" changes are wrought which physical means fail to accomplish. But here our account would end if this were an adequate explanation. Our reason for telling about the marvellous result accomplished in this young man's life is found in the fact that the change was more than victory over death and the successful staying of a disease presumably fatal. It will hardly be possible to see the meaning of this profound turning of a young life from one channel into another if we look at it as a mental cure. The change was the equivalent of a conversion and much more, if by a conversion we mean the adoption of a creed which makes of a worldly man a follower of Christ. For this young man had already given himself to Christ. Strange to relate, in adopting the teachings of the new therapeutist he renounced the church as an organization, together with all its observances, also his desire to become a minister. Yet on the other hand he became more faithfully a follower of Christ than before.

The apparent paradox is resolved when we note that the transition was from the Calvinistic deity to faith in God as immanent, loving, guiding Father, immediate and accessible, in a sense as intimate as that of our own self-consciousness when aware that there is an ideal self within us, when we will to have that self become actual in daily life. It meant the conviction that the true God is already present in our spirit to uplift and make us free as rapidly as we come to recognize and respond, admitting the divine life into all parts of our being. It signified the disclosure of the original gospel of health and freedom taught and proved by the Master. Sectarian Christianity no longer existed for him. He reacted against its limitations as against the faults of medical science and practice. Yet he did not in any sense cease to believe in Christ as the true Saviour of the world.

That his was a genuine conversion in the practical sense of the word was shown by the fact that, once restored to active service, he began to live by what to him was a new gospel and to give his time to spreading this gospel in the world. We naturally look for different signs if we gain this point of view, and we are not surprised when we find a person somewhat critical of the old order of thought. For the reaction, in the case of a man who discards theology as a formulated scheme but retains religion, is in favor of what is spiritually essential. It is constructive and worthy of being regarded from within. Intellectually it is critical because the understanding must be clarified. Spiritually it assimilates all that was best in the type of thought that has been discarded.

Later, our young man was fond of saying that one must set aside all preconceptions for the time being, to grasp the new point of view as a "spiritual science." So we too must neglect for the moment ideas which are familiar and toward which we strongly incline, if we shall enter sympathetically into a spirit of truth capable of giving a creative impetus in Christian life. This is not easy for those who judge by doctrines in contrast with experience disclosing new fields.

This gospel involved the idea that Christ is not a Person in the sense in which orthodox believers associate the Son with the Father in the Trinity. The leading idea was that Christ was divine wisdom taught and exemplified by the historical personality, Jesus of Nazareth, whom we begin truly to understand when we make this discrimination. The extent to which such a distinction is justifiable by interpretation of the Gospels is a question which we postpone for the time being. We are now concerned with its practical consequences through belief in "the light of Christ in the soul," the living Christ near to the heart of every sincere believer, the divine wisdom and love made concrete in our needs and aspirations.

Much depends on our prior thought concerning the human self. If instead of regarding man as "fallen" or dwelling upon his shortcomings and his sins, pitying him in his miserable plight and emphasizing the need of supernatural salvation, we hold that man is by birthright free and sound, yet at first ignorant and in need of experience which shall make him aware of resident divine powers within him, we are ready for the proposition that Christ is the enlightenment needed to awaken man to his true estate. For man's miseries are unwittingly of his own making, ignorant that he is a spirit endowed with power in the image and likeness of God. These miseries belong with man's lesser selfhood when, under bondage to material sense, he is like one sleeping. Even our young man with all his Christian zeal was as one in a dream. To awaken him was to give him a different idea of what it means to be faithful to the Master, to believe in God and live by the divine wisdom. It was to start from within in the living present, the divine moment of his true selfhood. It was to concentrate upon what man is ideally, touched with the fulness of life by the quickening presence of Christ.

History virtually disappears from this point of view and one sees the living Christ coming through the mists with a glad message of light and freedom. Whatever is deemed noblest and best is already here. This was the real purport of the Gospels, that we should find the living Christ now. This means an ever-present resource, for power, for health, for life wherewith to break down barriers which imprison souls and set them free. It does not mean the exaltation of the self, as if one claimed for the man of today what the wisest men of the ages have missed.

It does not mean undue emphasis on inner experience, as if in one's egotism one attributed all power to finite man. Yet it certainly does mean an application of ancient truth which has eluded good and wise men. It gives every one, however humble his station, however great his trouble, opportunity to begin where he is and live by the science which Jesus taught when summoning men to fulness of being.

The impressive characteristic of the healer who restored our young man was constructive humility, an exceptional combination of true receptivity interposing no obstacle and an affirmativeness reaching beyond what ordinary Christians venture to claim. This is vastly different from attributing all virtue to the finite self. It calls for much more thorough renovation of one's life than is usually expected by priest or physician, each of whom ordinarily asks us to reform but half a man. It means taking life seriously indeed, yet with a joy, a benefit, a freedom, with powers of service beyond comparison.

Our young man began to reform the whole man—he who needed it less in most respects than many men do. Or, rather the Spirit wrought such regeneration in him. The Spirit summoned him to live a consistent life in mind and body. He was still handicapped, with his frail physique and difficult inheritance. But he began anew to work on and up. He led a triumphant life of the spirit. That is the great consideration.

Too often we judge a human life by its failures, by disfigurements and injuries which do not wholly disappear, by apparent lapses and inconsistencies. We should gain the point of view of the achieving spirit, taking up one phase of life after another as steadily as each can be understood and brought into line. The perfect demonstration will come only when the entire human race is regenerated. No one can truly know himself in the profounder sense save as a member of a human family whose weaknesses and ignorance he shares when he starts on the long road. No one can begin truly to be free unless he extends a helping hand to fellow mortals. Indeed, one may begin thus genuinely to serve while struggling to get on one's feet out of quagmires of inheritance which seem overwhelming.

The spiritual life is a progress, not a leap. What one claims who adopts Christ as guide, in preference to sciences and methods which approach man from the outside, is that the wisdom which proves itself by its works here and now can be carried on to the perfect demonstration.

Our young man had all the obstacles he could contend with during years when people were not ready for the truth he saw. But these were given him, let us say, not to make light of, not to run away from, but to face, to call out his courage and his faith, that he might learn the law of Christ, live by it and help others to live by it. His spirit could not have begun to be supreme save through obstacles in the flesh and his environment over which to become triumphant. The turning-point came with him when he realized that infinite resources of divine love and wisdom were ready at hand within him.

What we need to do, therefore, to realize the power of the Spirit in the Christ-consciousness is to discern the elements or principles which are active in this triumph. For we have to do with a more enlightened idea of the human spirit, a different view of health extending into the spiritual life in its fulness, and an interpretation of healing adapted to the deepest problems of the soul.

We are apt to think when we believe rightly that the rest will follow, as zealous Christians have thought all through the ages, with their doctrine of "faith alone." We are apt to think that it is sufficient to see near-by causes of our unhappiness, and make some slight change. But a spiritual interpretation of life calls upon us to trace matters to the end, not stopping with merely remedial activities.

The finding of the way back to health is

secondary to the discovery of the kind of life we might have lived had we always kept close to God, had we drawn upon divine resources, practised divine wisdom, manifested divine love, outwardly as well as inwardly in spiritual health. The power of the spirit *to keep the way,* to live by the truth, attain the life, is a greater consideration than the power to regain the way when we have missed it. For Christ is affirmative in us. The Christ is the true science of right living, and only indirectly the corrective of our errors. We are bidden to judge by the ideal, the normal, and to expand our life to its full proportions. We are bidden to find the kingdom which is within and to live by its law. This the power of the Spirit is able to accomplish through us. This gives the impetus which makes daily life a joy in the presence of our friends and our God.

II

THE PRICELESS POSSESSION

DESPITE the impressiveness of such a transition in the spiritual life as the one we have considered in the foregoing, onlookers have not as yet been persuaded to follow as far as one could wish. The reasons for this conservatism are worth noting before we turn to a restatement of the central principles.

To the average observer this new interest has meant little more than discovery of the power of thought and the hitherto concealed functions of the subconscious mind. We have all heard about suggestion by this time and have learned to make use of it in dealing with our fellow men. We know about the subconscious mind, and we take it into account when explaining experiences once attributed to mysterious forces outside the human personality. Whatever may be thought about mental healing as a specific for all illnesses, we all acknowledge that our power over life has increased by the addition of this new interest. Here, however, the matter often ends, and the therapeutic movement is regarded as one more new cult assigned to its proper place.

The advocates of mental healing have been partly responsible for this. For much has been said and written about the utility of thought as a more direct way of securing success, as if success in material things were the chief end of life. Hence there has been a tendency to concentrate upon the psychology of success. The new interest could hardly mean more than this to people who had no genuine desire to alter their mode of life, who wanted to find a quicker way of being relieved of their ills while retaining most of their pleasures, habits and social occupations.

Then, too, there has been a tendency to regard the new spiritual science as a kind of absolutism admitting of no appeal. To make this claim in behalf of the authority of a text-book is of course to miss the whole point, that each soul has power to draw upon immanent divine sources according to need. Thus people have turned aside in favor of an organization which might have pressed forward to the new revelation of Christianity.

In all movements this is likely to be the case for a time. Only a few adopt a new master's teaching with adequate seriousness. We have had leaders and visions enough in the history of our race to make us children of light. What the majority want is to be free from pain and misery due to their excesses, that they may be a little more prudent, and retain their old life as fully as possible. Consequently, when any one comes forward with assurance that we can become unselfish friends of man and worthy sons of God we turn away as did the rich young man, mindful of our luxuries. Creatures of habit, imitative, conservative and envious, we refuse to adopt a plan of action which will reach to the uttermost confines of our social kingdom and summon us to be noblemen of the Spirit.

The simple truth is that all our illnesses, woes and vices are intimately related, and that really to be rid of one is to overcome all. It is not a question of gaining enough insight into the power of the human spirit to overcome a few maladies, and then disregard material things and laws as if they did not exist. The power of the spirit is not a half-way measure. It is not disclosed that we may do as we like. The real test of our spiritual faith is given us when we carry the spiritual life into every sphere of our natural and social interests. The power of our human spirit was given us to live by the Spirit. This Spirit has become manifest in this splendid world of space and time, objective in bodies and things, and the Spirit's manifestations are not to be ignored.

Life is surrounded by conditions intended to

call the human spirit into power. Our souls need to be tested to the full, and the tests are distributed along the line of life that we may meet them one by one, through divine guidance, and gradually grow into supremacy. The conditions we face and must conquer are from the self-same Spirit which gives us power to become victors. But these conditions seen in the divine light prove to be friendly. Life is indeed friendly through and through. There is no offsetting Power whose forces we must conquer in order to live the spiritual life. In our ignorance we have mistaken friends for foes, and acted toward nature as if matter were the product of some alien Energy striving to circumvent us, instead of a vehicle for the manifestation of Spirit. This is the whole problem of life as the new therapeutism regards it: to convert apparent enemies to friends and learn to live with nature in our well-ordered bodies as true children of Spirit.

The pioneers in this field were no more favored than other mortals. They had to work their way along year by year and prove the spiritual law for themselves. They did not come by their exceptional wisdom through "revelation." Indeed the word revelation is illusory if we mean wisdom put into our minds apart from the spiritual growth which discloses and proves it. Human experience as a whole is a revelation to him who has eyes. Christianity came as the culminating clue to this experience which we all know. Its newness consisted not so much in its ideas as in the transfiguring life and works of the Master through whose service for humanity God became manifest in fulness.

We may say in brief that the one great reason why the world has not whole-heartedly adopted this new version of Christianity is found in the fact that this preliminary period was needed to bring us back to the Gospel. The pioneers cleared the way. They planted the new seed. Its fruitage was judged by appearances. Now we are learning that what seemed to be a mental device for winning people was in reality a call "to live the life." The requisite change of thought from the old order to the new was only a beginning. The psychology of success was merely an aspect of spiritual truths including the whole of life. Behind it all there was a priceless possession which the few caught sight of and have been cherishing. What was that priceless possession? Can we put it into words?

It was the truth of the Inward Presence once more made known to men. It was the rediscovery, made ever and again in human history, that there is in man a God-sense or power of direct communion with heavenly realities, such that experience is the test and verification of all spiritual wisdom. In a practical way this means that any man at any time, whatever his need, may lift his problem into heavenly light and see it transfigured by the guidance he needs. It means further that this light may be admitted into our whole nature, that there is guidance for every need whatsoever. And the application of this guidance to healing was the special phase which this wisdom brought us at first, because this truth needed to be restored to the world. This truth brought back, it became possible to regard the Gospel in its fulness anew. Thus the way to "live the life" again opened before men as they had not seen it for ages.

The experience of the first pioneer in this rediscovery shows that any one might make the same discovery—guided by the Spirit. For the heavenly light is always shining. What was needed to bring men to knowledge of it through quest for healing was a method of meditation or silent realization. This method was acquired by our pioneers through the prior discovery that man has inner senses or intuitive power enabling him to discern spiritual reality. All men have evidences of such inward power, but only a few put the evidences together to see that our spiritual nature is adapted for manifold use when we need power in any field. What is needed is an experience sufficiently absorbing so that we will follow it through and find the Spirit within the human spirit, the Lord of life presiding over our human life.

Many of us arrive naturally enough at the point where prayer spontaneously takes expression on our lips, and we realize that the power of prayer has never reached its limits with us. There are many believers in the inward light as the direct witness of the Spirit, the true reason for worship. Every earnest Christian has some experience of inward piety akin to divine love. We all believe that "the pure in heart" shall see God. But there is a further step which seems almost as new, as if no one had the habit of prayer, none believed in the inward light or purity of heart. This step is into knowledge of the Inward Presence *as power*. It shows one how to enter into quickening Life through vivid realization of the love and the wisdom that are ours. It shows the way to a dynamic experience passing beyond mere meditation or worship. Realization is more detailed than prayer as most men know prayer. It enlists ideals made vivid and held before the mind. It is concerned with specific needs, with the conviction that the life made concrete through concentration will begin at once to take effect.

Such realization becomes possible when the mind gives itself to the belief that our human spirit is rightfully an instrument of God, heir to divine wisdom, an immediate participant in the Inward Presence.

Such realization also differs from prayer because it implies an experienced contrast between the inner mind and the outer, between one plane of consciousness and another. We are all famiiliar with the contrast between the two voices or natures. Many of us know what it is to feel free or to feel conditioned. We know that there is a difference between an ideal and a mere process. In a way each of us has his two worlds of thought. But we have not all learned to bring these ideas together so that our inner world is a meeting-point between the spirit and a higher activity which can be utilized when there is need. We have not learned to break away from externalizing consciousness at will. We have no definite idea what the activity is within us which makes the change. We have not learned to be alone with God's ideal.

It is fairly easy to acquire merely psychological knowledge of this contrast. Some effort is required to pass beyond all mental devices, penetrating behind all mental appearances to spiritual reality. The priceless possession is intimacy of relation through spiritual experience in which the Inward Presence becomes an immediate source of guidance and power. This experience means more than the coming of a vision or mystical ecstasy which the participant neither understands nor is able to recover. It may be the same in kind as the better sort of mystical experience, while calling for a much more intelligible interpretation.

This experience of the Inward Presence is recoverable through understanding of the conditions. Such understanding is accessible to every one who is willing to entertain the idea of immediate experience of the presence of God in contrast with the tradition in the churches that only through zealously guarded authority can man approach God. It becomes possible when we take seriously the idea that man is spirit and is recipient of Life ready to make him in fulness a child of God in image and likeness.

This inward quest might lead to self-centeredness if it were not for the experienced contrast between the inner mind and the outer. To enter more deeply into one's mere self is not to find the inner mind at all. The priceless possession is awareness of the Inward Presence by being in the sanctuary of the Spirit where a higher light is shining. The kingdom is "at hand," it is "within," it comes "without observation," bearing its own evidences, summoning man to seek it first and last. The particular self making the quest is secondary. The essential is the great gift made to the self seeking the Presence in all sincerity and devotion.

According to the old order of thought life was a warfare. Hence the Gospel was put in negative form. It seemed necessary to begin by condemning and resisting, as if one were struggling with an alien Power. In the new order we find that a different attitude transforms the same forces once deemed hostile. The alleged enemy disappears in the divine light shining from above. There is only friendliness and peace, with a Life ever present that is working for health and freedom. Even the world seems to have faded for the moment. To have the world given back is to have it bestowed as God's world.

To rise to the level of this higher light is to find oneself in a measure a spokesman of the Spirit speaking to the spirit in other men. Such speech is given us through pure disinterestedness, when love touches the heart and the human self interposes no obstacle. That is why one may venture to call this the voice of the living Christ, the healing Christ summoning others to come into the same communion with the Father. Not until the self thus becomes an instrument have we seen what the universal reign of the Gospel on earth might be. It is we who have been chosen, not that we attained the end by mere self-consciousness. Our part is to prepare the way as best we can for this consecration, with the hope that we may be chosen disciples of the living Lord.

The central principle is that there is but one Wisdom and all spiritual truth comes from this source, that there is guidance for each need, a wisdom which sees the state of the soul as it truly is. Our part is to lift the Spirit to the level of that Wisdom, that its guidance may become our light on the path, its leading the one we follow through every vicissitude. Otherwise put, there is one Love and all genuine devotion on our part is a sharing of its compassion, its tenderness and power to do good. There is love for each heart. Love is the great healing power, touching the soul, quickening, opening, stirring into strength, and making the soul a radiating centre.

No words can adequately tell what knowledge of this priceless possession means for the individual. He who would gain it must first entertain the idea of such unison with Life, then see what leadings come, what there is in the self and in daily life to impede. It is not the idea but experience itself which gives the reality, when there is a need which opens the spirit to seek and find, to receive and give. What the printed word may do is to suggest the way. There is no formula that will unlock the inner secrets. The way of the heart is more interior. But affirmation will help us toward purity of heart and the guidance which leads into "the way." If we had kept the open vision the way would immediately disclose itself. Experience is given us that we may regain this vision, learning anew to see things as they are, as the Spirit illuminates them.

There are moments when the Spirit seems to possess us, to imbue us with power and cast over our being its soft radiance. Cherishing these beatific moments when they come, never trying to control them, we find that the way is disclosed to the next experience. That way followed, the succeeding moments will appear, and all experience will seem in truth a divine revelation. Outward life as it unfolds from moment to moment will then assume its proper place as means of expression and means of testing what the Spirit has disclosed. It is everything to know that the real work is that of the Spirit in us, whatever part man appears to play. The human spirit is akin to the divine and can conform to the Spirit's leadings. It is also within man's power to be led into freedom in detail and at large, out of every anxiety, fear, friction, inertia, rebellion, or whatever the state may be that impedes. Spirit is ready to set us free when we say the word.

To see what this priceless possession means for those who believe in spiritual healing as a consequence of the spiritual life, we need to reconsider the Gospel in the light of the distinction widely accepted among disciples of this method, the distinction between Jesus and the Christ. This distinction meant everything to the pioneers, since the whole method of healing turned upon recognition of "the Christ within." The contrast grew up around the idea of the inner self as immediately open to the Inward Presence which experience itself revealed. It was not a theoretical contrast. It is not meant to be a basis for theology or for creeds. Consequently one is asked to set doctrinal matters aside for the time being and turn to the Gospels with this clue from inner experience. There need be no loss in so doing, for a person may freely return to the idea of the Lord which has proved its value in the spiritual life. One is simply asked to follow where the living Christ may lead today, that the glorious message of the Comforter may be fully given to men. Those who have caught the new vision believe they have a priceless possession because they find it disclosing love, wisdom and power unknown even to those who accept the Gospel in full as a historical and doctrinal message, as the foundation of the Church. For they have caught a vision of the Church Universal over and above all sects and creeds. And in catching this vision they have found the test of its reality in "the life."

III

THE CHRIST

"And many other signs truly did Jesus in the presence of his disciples, which are not written in this book. But these are written, that ye might believe that Jesus is the Christ, the Son of God; and that believing ye might have life through his name."—John xx, 30, 31.

Two sharply contrasted views concerning Christ have prevailed, the one that Jesus was the unique Son of God from eternity, wholly perfect and entirely divine; the other that he as a man attained the wisdom and power indicated in the Gospels as any one might strive to realize a spiritual ideal. The one errs by overemphasis on the divine, leaves no room for temptations and victories as we know them. The other assigns such importance to the human self that it fails to account for the universal wisdom and the far-reaching love of the Christ. Nor is the situation improved when we try to adopt one of those elusive midway positions which stand, now for the divine, and now for the human, but which afford no clear idea of the divine as manifested in the human according to a universal ideal. We seem to be imposing our own limitations on the Christ when we conceive of the wisdom and love displayed by Jesus as results of merely finite endeavor. What we need is an approach which does not intrude upon the infinite but yields the conviction that through the incarnation the divine love and wisdom dwelt with men in a human self not too far removed from the imperfections which we know.

We may begin by regarding the Christ as universal divine love and wisdom, taking our clue from the Gospels as they read. Such a reading of the Gospels is possible if we deem the recorded words parts only of the eternal Word of God, written in the hearts and minds of men throughout the ages. If the Christ is universal, surely no statement in any book can limit this wisdom so that there shall be nothing more to say.

Anyone reading the Gospels without theological predispositions must admit that there is a prevailing contrast between passages which pertain to the historical Jesus and those that imply special claims in his behalf as Messiah, Christ, the Lord. By the term "the Christ" we shall here mean Messiahship or Christhood, however it may be interpreted. If Jesus were "merely human," as some say, the special claims would seem preposterous indeed. If these claims bespeak the Christ or universal divine love and wisdom, they involve the conviction that God has a universal way of making Himself known to men.

The difficulty usually encountered rests on the fact that Jesus speaks sometimes as man struggling to be faithful, and sometimes as love or wisdom implying all faith and all triumphs. Distinguishing between the personality and the love or wisdom for the moment, we may consider those passages which would be almost devoid of meaning unless we should think of the Christ as universal. Note how numerous are those passages which look beyond the man who speaks to the universal principle which he teaches.

"He that loveth father or mother more than me is not worthy of me; and he that loveth son or daughter more than me is not worthy of me. And he that doth not take up his cross and follow after me, is not worthy of me. He that findeth his life shall lose it; and he that loseth his life for my sake shall find it" (Matt. x, 37-39). "He that receiveth you receiveth me, and he that receiveth me receiveth him that sent me" (x, 40). "Come unto me, all ye that labor and are heavy laden, and I will give you rest. Take my yoke upon you, and learn of me; for

I am meek and lowly in heart: and ye shall find rest unto your souls" (xi, 28, 29). The wisdom thus speaking is declared to be greater than the temple, greater than Solomon or Jonah, and "Lord of the Sabbath." This wisdom was prior to the historical incarnation, it is one with the Father in the works and teachings recorded in the Gospels, and is able to be with the disciples always, "even unto the end of the world."

The Gospel of John from first to last expresses this universal wisdom in such a way that it can hardly be identified with or limited to a personality in a certain time or place. It is first associated with the Word, then with the Light both in the sense of the enlightenment of every man born into the world and also in the sense of life. Then follow passages in which the Christ is brought before us as "the living water" which quenches the thirst of men, as the bread of life which shall appease all hunger even unto the life eternal, as the flesh and blood which symbolize the immortal spirit, the divine plenitude, and other passages which have no meaning unless understood universally. The Christ as thus brought vividly before us in the greatest incidents recorded in the Gospels is indeed the universal Giver of life, the way, the truth, the surpassing power, triumphing over death, over space and time, over all limitations or conditions.

"And Jesus said unto them, I am the bread of life: he that cometh unto me shall never hunger; and he that believeth on me shall never thirst. . . . This is the bread that cometh down from heaven. . . . I am come that they might have life, and that they might have it more abundantly. . . . I am the resurrection and the life: he that believeth in me, though he were dead, yet shall he live. . . . And I, if I be lifted up from the earth will draw all men unto me. . . . I am the way, the truth, and the life: no man cometh unto the Father but by me."

Then follow still more intimate passages in which Jesus, while speaking in part as a person, utters statements which could be true only of a universal spirit or principle. Thus we have the figure of the vine as the symbol of all effective life in the Spirit, all true discipleship and service. The Christ is here a principle such that it can abide in all who are faithful to the precepts and the love set before the disciples as an ideal. It is not alone the spirit manifested in Jesus in his fidelity to the Father, but one capable of extension such that others shall receive it and abide in it. The self that speaks is not limited to the man of flesh and blood.

"I am the true vine, and my Father is the

husbandman. . . . Abide in me, and I in you. . . . I am the vine, ye are the branches. . . . If ye abide in me, and my words abide in you, ye shall ask what ye will, and it shall be done unto you. . . . Herein is my Father glorified, that ye bear much fruit. . . . As the Father hath loved me, so I love you: continue ye in my love."

Even this the infinitely tender thought of the love which is symbolized by the vine is surpassed in the great prayer of the seventeenth chapter. For here Jesus is speaking to the disciples in statements addressed to the Father expressive of a oneness which is not the oneness of identity, nor that of two beings whose association is unique; but the spiritual relationship which may become true of all.

"Neither pray I for these alone, but for them also that shall believe on me through their word; that they all may be one; as thou, Father, art in me, and I in thee, that they also may be one in us; that the world may believe that thou hast sent me. And the glory which thou gavest me I have given them: that they may be one, even as we are; I in them, and thou in me, that they may be perfected into one." The "I" or being who here speaks also says, "for thou lovedst me before the foundation of the world." It is not a temporal self or merely historical being who speaks. A spirit or life is here expressed which can bring all men together who receive spiritual life as Jesus speaks of his oneness with the Father. This passage carries our thought back to that of the apparently unqualified statement of Chapter X in which Jesus says, "I and my Father are one."

This saying is often taken to mean the absolute identity of the historical person Jesus with the Father, and it is put with the passage in Chapter XIV in which Jesus says, "He that hath seen me hath seen the Father," with the understanding that the two are absolutely one. But this passage in Chapter X is followed by the explanatory statement, ". . . the Father is in me, and I in him." In the sense of this surpassing truth Jesus now prays that all may be one, "as thou, Father, art in me, and I in thee, that they also may be one in us." Plainly the oneness refers to unity of spirit in universal wisdom. We are to understand the figure of the vine and the branches as a symbol implying ineffable nearness which no words can express but which the heart knows; not as an exact theological statement involving absolute identity of substance.

Christ then is a unifying spirit or life which brings men into the most intimate relationship with the divine love, the relationship of Father to son, Master to disciple, disciple to disciple as brother with brother, and thus ever on and on as far as this love shall be preserved in its purity. This supreme relationship brings to completion the promises of the preceding chapters in which the Christ is symbolized as the door, the light, the truth, the way, and the life, each one being universal. These characteristics are never mentioned in an exclusive sense, but always with reference to the power going forth, the bond of union, the guiding wisdom. We are not led into a confined and narrow world when Jesus assures us that no man comes to the Father save through him, for he is speaking of the universal way, truth, and life, the way of the Christ. "All things are delivered unto me of my Father: and no man knoweth the Son, but the Father; neither knoweth any man the Father, save the Son, and he to whomsoever the Son will reveal him" (Matt. xi, 27). The power speaking is at once the bread, the blood, the resurrection, the life, the light, the way, and the truth. Each of these is universal, and only through the Christ may they be understood. Each of these is given that men may have life more abundantly. "I am the resurrection and the life . . . because I live ye shall live also." All men thus knowing and living by the Christ will be quickened.

Again, we note the clearness of vision and surety of knowledge with which Jesus performs works of healing and other "mighty works." These are plainly not the works of one who performs miracles or mysteries, as if by special privilege and by the aid of concealed powers. He who performs these works proceeds as one who knows precisely what he is doing and why, who grasps the implied laws and understands the forces employed. They are works given by the Father for the Master to do, as bearing witness that the Father has sent the Son (John v, 36). Thus they have intelligible meaning, and the disciples, if unable fully to understand, are bidden to believe "for the very works' sake." The efficient principle is not only stated, namely, that the Father dwelling in the Master does the works; but assurance is given that those who believe shall perform such works also. The disciples had already been sent forth to perform similar works, with explicit instructions concerning this form of spiritual service.

It might confidently be said therefore that the works were wrought according to a spiritual science, so that Jesus could foretell the accomplishing of greater works when this science should be more extensively applied. That is, these works were wrought out in the open, in the light of divine truth universal in scope and meaning, for the purpose of making that truth known which brings spiritual freedom and establishes the kingdom of God in the minds and hearts of men. Hence Jesus said to critics who sought to turn the matter aside from the main principle, "But if I by the spirit of God cast out devils, then is the kingdom of God come upon you" (Matt. xii, 28).

Furthermore, the extent of the principle is shown by the fact that these works involve the overcoming of all the adversities to which the flesh is subject in man's ignorance of the power of the spirit. The carrying out of the principle involves the mastery of diseases of all kinds, the casting out of obsessions, and the overcoming of death as death is understood by those who know not the power of the spirit. The emphasis is everywhere put on the life or spirit which overcomes, just as in the case of the crucifixion and resurrection the emphasis belongs on the triumphant life which the Master lived. There is a fundamental difference between occult power which an adept might acquire and display through magic, and a universal spiritual science implying divine laws capable of being understood through interior enlightenment. The first calls for special training in arts which man has acquired, arts which even the unprincipled might employ; the second calls for a consecrated life into which man is guided by divine light in his soul.

The same fidelity to a principle over and above special privileges is shown in passages in which Jesus, refusing to allow any credit to be given, invariably refers to works given him to do, words given him to speak, light to be made manifest, truth that will bestow freedom. No words could be more emphatic than the utterances of Jesus in this connection. "And he said unto him, Why callest thou me good? there is none good but one, that is, God" (Matt. xix, 17). "The Son can do nothing of himself, but what he seeth the Father do . . . I can of mine own self do nothing: as I hear, I judge: and my judgment is just; because I seek not mine own will, but the will of the Father who hath sent me. . . . If I bear witness of myself, my witness is not true. . . . There is another that beareth witness of me. . . . I am come in my Father's name. . . . My doctrine is not mine, but his that sent me. . . . I do nothing of myself; but as my Father hath taught me, I speak these things."

These are not the words of one who takes credit unto himself. When Jesus says, "Before Abraham was, I am;" "Search the scriptures . . . they are they which testify of me;" "Come unto me all ye that labor and are heavy laden," he is plainly not calling the weary and distressed to him as a man only. Jesus teaches from first to last that all wisdom, life and power have a single source. It is the Father who gives according to our needs, who guides us along life's pathway, who sustains, provides, bestows life and light. All the words of wisdom proceed from Him. The works of healing are His. It is His mission that saves, quickens and establishes the kingdom. The divine plan of this mission antedates Abraham. Jesus fulfils it step by step, that all things may be accomplished according to divine law, that the human may not intrude. Hence he is able to say without qualification that he is faithful in word and deed to the Father's will. He knows that the Father's love and wisdom are so disclosed that the disciples actually hear and see the Father in the Son: ". . . and the word which ye hear is not mine, but the Father's who sent me." "He that hath seen me, hath seen the Father. . . . The Father and I are one." It is these statements which disclose to us the Christ, which show that a universal wisdom and love were made manifest in Jesus.

We may state the universal principle as follows: There is one right attitude toward the Father, whose wisdom and love constitute the real efficiency in the minds and hearts of men, namely, that we should seek first the purpose or forward movement of the divine life in process through us, adopting this the divine trend of life as our own, serving and living with the realization that it is the Father who accomplishes in each of us the work He would have us do. Jesus is the living representative who not only teaches but proves this Christ-wisdom which he came to bring to men. As exemplifier of the Gospel he turns attention away from himself. We must "see the Christ stand," saying with John the Baptist, "Behold the Lamb of God." We should discern the universality of the way, the truth, and the life. The Christ-wisdom is in a sense separable and capable of being taught by itself. Having discerned this universal principle, we are ready to consider the selfhood of God as Father on the one side and the personality of Jesus in the historic sense on the other.

The practical consequences are plain. We have beforc us a universal spiritual science involving "the way, the truth, and the life." We know its source, the universality of its provisions, and of the guidances accessible to each. We know that no man alone can save his fellow men, that the true Saviour is God the Father, is the Christ. This wisdom is in a sense over and above each one of us as a person, inasmuch as we may all abide in the divine love as branches of the true vine. Hence it includes not only all men as sons of God, but the Father too; it is the abiding relationship throughout all eternity.

We may then say unqualifiedly that Christ is divine; not merely "the anointed one," or the enlightened one, but enlightenment itself. Hence we see the value and meaning of impersonal forms of expression, such as the spirit of truth, the Comforter, the Holy Spirit. This is the universal element foreseen in the Scriptures as a whole. All spiritual history points forward to it. It is discoverable, at any time when men receive the essential enlightenment. It speaks as it were to all men, in all time, this central word of appeal reaching beyond all historical events: "Behold, I stand at the door and knock." "No man cometh unto the Father but by me." "Neither doth any know the Father save the Son, and he to whomsoever the Son willeth to reveal him." "I am the door: by me if any man enter in, he shall be saved, and shall go in and out and find pasture."

IV

TRUE SPIRITUAL SCIENCE

"AND ye shall know the truth, and the truth shall make you free. . . . If the Son . . . shall make you free, ye shall be free indeed."—John viii, 32, 36.

What is the Christ or universal wisdom taught by the Master in the Gospels, and how does it differ from other sciences? It is a higher science pertaining to the inner life of man as part of the whole mission of Jesus in making known the kingdom of God on earth. It does not start with the discovery and observation of external facts, then work up to knowledge of natural laws through inference and criticism, as we proceed when fostering such a science as physics or biology; it begins with a certain appeal to the heart of man in behalf of an invisible realm of being in which he has his real existence. The test of its power or truth is not in its mere law or rational consistency, in the ability of man to think it out to the end and defend it against all objections; but in its application to human needs, through the works accomplished by it. Hence its first appeal is to the individual to live by it, see its truth for himself, become free himself, that he may be quickened to carry the liberating message to others. It is the divine wisdom descending into the human spirit and proving itself practical, workable, concrete; then working out into social life and the physical organism, that it may be shown in all its completeness or objectivity. This divine science therefore proves itself by taking shape in the concrete deeds of men, the word made flesh in thought, in will and in life, when it becomes a fact; whereas the natural sciences value facts first and only by laborious thinking arrive at universals.

It might of course be said that from the first Jesus has the social aim in view, that his one great interest is brotherhood or service. But since it is the individual doing his true work who stands for the social ideal, we find Jesus everywhere beginning with individual men and summoning them to a life of wholeness or all-round health. Jesus addresses individuals whose needs are typical, meanwhile setting forth principles which enable us to see what is the true panacea. The standard of health as we thus find it taught point by point involves three great essentials. First, there must be integrity within the self, oneness of purpose between head and heart, constancy in serving one master, with all that this unity implies by way of purity of motive, courage and persistence in pursuing the one ideal. This means loving the Father above all men and above the world, believing in the divine way of life with its provisions for daily welfare; and carrying this faith into the little affairs which even more than the great contests of life show what we truly believe. In the second place, there should be love of the neighbor expressed in concrete service proving its truth and reality by deeds, with the love of Christ first in order, whatever may be the love for father, mother, brother; a losing of selfish or lesser nature to find the unselfish or greater. And, in the third place, there should be outward or physical health proving that a man lives by the Christ in fulness or integrity, instead of limiting his interests to a narrow field or a special theory.

In seeking these ends Jesus strikes at the root of every life not founded on this unity within the self. He singles out hypocrisy and self-righteousness as typical of the wrong mode of life in general. Why does he single out these two? Because they stand for appearances contrary to man's real inner life. Until a man begins to display in outward conduct what he truly is within, as little as he may have actually attained, he is unable to begin the constructive life, there is war between forces within him, and he slips back in one direction while striving to make headway in another. The hypocrite may, for example, pretend to be living a pure upright life as regards matters in the social world while seeking self-gratification in other ways usually thrown out of account. The self-righteous man may deem himself spiritual, therefore "saved," because he believes what Christ is said to teach concerning salvation by those who separate between sin and the problems of health. But the Master combines and teaches that which followers have separated. When he heals or forgives he uses essentially the same language: "Thy sins be forgiven thee," or, "Arise and walk." That is to say, disease, whatever its external conditions or occasions, arises from disordered life. There is no permanent cure save through purification within the life of every desire or activity, from lust to self-centredness in its most refined forms, which interferes with the free expression of the divine image of health. Sin, whatever the ostensible motives and social consequences, arises from disordered life. There is no salvation save through cleansing the entire "inside of the cup," including those conditions which make for disease. To have sins "forgiven," or to be made whole of one's disease, is to begin to live in such a way that neither the germs of sin nor conditions that invite disease shall find fertile soil.

The one is the other so far as the inner life is concerned. For the Master is not talking about symptoms, nor is he referring to the outward occasions of disease or the semblances of sin. He is speaking of causes, hence of the mode of life which shall cleanse man through and through. This has been a hard saying for the world. Men have wanted to believe with their lips for the sake of the soul's future welfare, while living as they liked in the world and attributing their illnesses and sorrows, their unhappiness and miseries to outward things not supposed to be important.

We observe that Jesus does not apply his science by taking away the effects of sin or outward manifestations of disease, as if this sufficed to save the soul. He strikes at the root of the tree and bids his followers emulate him, despite all the pretenses of the hypocritical and self-righteous. We note, for example, that he seeks faith on the part of both individuals and groups, that he goes where faith prevails, commends men and women displaying faith, and tells what faith will accomplish. "According to your faith be it unto you," or "Thy faith hath made thee whole," is his general mode of expression. By faith he plainly means much more than intellectual acceptance, dependence on the divine providence or trust for the future. He calls for a mode of life in the living present which makes for wholeness. Such faith is constructive, it implies the affirmative attitude with its emphasis on life and what life brings. To have faith is "to enter into life," and to enter into life is to turn each of those elements in our nature whereby we oppose the divine incoming life into elements of harmony and oneness. To have faith is to believe in the divine image and likeness, and to do one's best to live by it in the little passing thoughts, the minor motives or sentiments. True faith springs "out of the abundance of the heart," in openness of spirit.

Again, we note that in applying this science Jesus seeks the needy, "the poor in spirit," the afflicted, the lost sheep; and that he readily associates with publicans and sinners, sitting at meat with them, and meeting their needs as individuals. "They that be whole need not a physician, but they that are sick." This outreaching in behalf of those who most need help leads one to believe that the test of spiritual science is its ability to solve difficult questions, which the world gives up on the ground that man is selfish and sensuous, burdened with fleshly appetites. If we are not to draw any such circle about the difficult and sinful, it must follow that we are not to condemn the sinner as a human spirit; but to summon him to the same fulness of life which is everywhere the resource of the Gospel.

Man's response to his physical appetites is in accordance with his affections or love. If he loves self first, he will seek those pleasures which spring from selfishness and his sins and the diseases springing from them will disclose self-love. To love others above self will be to seek those activities which express the true, full self through service. Thus everything depends in the last analysis on what man loves. Consequently Jesus addresses the affections and summons man to be his better, nobler self, "to go and sin no more," to take up his bed and walk, to be "every whit whole."

In the third place, we note that in carrying out this spiritual science Jesus not only seeks faith and turns first and last to those most in need, but seeks disciples who will go forth and labor in the vineyard as he has labored by meeting the world where it is. Jesus gave the disciples "power against unclean spirits to cast them out, and to heal all manner of sickness and all manner of disease." The Christ docs not merely bring the truth which sets them free, as if individual freedom were the goal of life. It does not simply teach men to pray, to preach, to discern the spirits of people, singling out those who are like houses divided against themselves; but quickens them with an efficient stirring love, and by making them "free indeed" inspires them to be active agents for the Christ wisdom. The power bestowed upon the disciple is not the power which he attains by himself through the practice of meditation, concentration or inner control; it does not spring from silence or receptivity alone; nor does it come through spiritual understanding apart by itself, as a product of study or the training of interior faculties. This power is like a gift, although universal in type—that is, a power bestowed by the Giver of life sending the disciple forth to give as freely as he has received.

Almost paradoxically this science bids man begin with himself and yet do anything rather than start with himself as if he could merely by taking thought become a Christ. The great truth that in and of himself man is naught and can accomplish nothing is so great, so deep, and far-reaching, that he who sees it has every reason in the world to anticipate profound consequences in his experience. Naturally then a large part of the Gospel is devoted to telling man how to begin with himself. Having begun to forgive, to cast out the beams that are in his own eye, to overcome anxiety and fear, to "let the dead bury their dead," man may acquire true receptivity. Having learned that both sin and sickness, so far as they spring from the life within him, have the same root, he would next ask, What then is my true self, when I am whole? If sickness be separateness, and sin be separateness, what part of me is not sick, what remains intact when I sin? This must be my inner selfhood or spirit, the child of God made in the divine image and likeness. I may say with confidence that my heavenly Father intended me to be sound and sane in all respects, and that in all my thinking and willing I should take this heavenly pattern as my standard, dwelling on the divine ideal. In my true self I am a child of light, a recipient of divine wisdom, open to divine love. This is the real source of health and of virtue. This source is within me, within every human soul, awaiting recognition and co-operation. The science of the Christ is above all the science of the true self.

What shall we say concerning inherited and external conditions which do not correspond with inner reality? What shall we do about manifestations of disease and sin which men minister to in the world? Shall we combat them too? Not in the same way by any means, if we understand the method of Christ. That method has been misinterpreted throughout the ages. It has been taken to mean the practice of the negative virtues, especially meekness, or non-resistance. But when we read the Gospels with open eyes, we find the Master taught a higher resistance, overcoming hate through loving our enemies, returning good for what is termed evil, the expression of righteous judgments in place of condemnation, and the outdoing of so-called virtuous people by freely giving as we would have others give unto us in times of equal need. Hence denial of the self does not mean self-sacrifice or the mortification of the flesh. The spirit indeed is willing while the flesh is weak, and there are manifold temptations to guard against. There are reasons for sacrifice on occasion. The great idea, however, is the conquering of the nature in us which inclines toward selfishness. The mastery of self is not by any means a negative consideration.

The Master does not turn into by-paths of endless discussion by contrasting the real with the unreal and developing a metaphysics founded on this contrast. He leaves this for those who care more for mere theory. Always he brings to man the condition, "If thou wilt enter into life," then do thus and so. The rest is death and need not be considered. His science turns upon truths which make for life. The way out of spiritual death is to have one Master, truth, or way; and to pursue this ideal with entire consecration. If thou wilt not enter into life, then receive the consequences of allegiance to riches, the world, self. For there is action and reaction whereby each man draws to himself what he loves. It is because what man loves is more central than what he thinks that Jesus directs attention to two great types of love. Thus it is borne in upon us with great conviction that the science which Jesus taught is the science of love to God and man.

It is hard for man to see that the way of the world is not the way of life, to see that intellectual rule may mean spiritual death, and that even when man has commanded all the forces of his natural environment which make for health he will not be truly sound and sane. Most men put the primary emphasis upon outward things, or if not they put it upon heredity, racial evil, human nature, or some other scapegoat. The Gospel bids man look to himself so decisively that he will never wish to turn his eyes anywhere else in the world.

The critic objects to this position, however. In an ideal world man might conquer his spirit, so it is said; under other conditions he might be unselfish, or truly free and wholly sound. But as matters are now we are all bound up with one another in ills and tribulations which we never bargained for, the innocent suffer with the guilty, and the individual can do little save to look out for himself, taking a little pleasure as he goes.

No, our science insists, it is not primarily a

question of heredity or environment, of handicaps or social relationships into which we are born. It is a question of the great eternal truth that man is a spirit born to mastery through divine love and wisdom in whose image and likeness he exists. There is no heredity so powerful as "our heredity from God." There is no environment equalling that of the divine resources more intimately at hand than any one knows. There is no condition so adverse that the spirit cannot begin forthwith to triumph over it. For the world exists for the sake of Spirit, the human spirit is clothed with a bodily organism as by a garment, and all things favor the man who lives by this great truth. We must start with the Spirit, think and live for the Christ, regarding the outward life as a sphere for the expression of spiritual things, if we would realize the full force of this science.

This is spiritual rather than mental science, because, having led the way to the inner life, it does not stop with mental attitudes, beliefs, anticipations and suggestions; but presses forward to the central statement that man's entire existence is involved, hence that if he would "enter into life" he must overcome everything in his nature that makes for selfishness with all its fruits in sins and illnesses. It is understood of course that as members of the human family we are all interrelated, so that we suffer with one another. It is understood that true health is social, and true life is social. But instead of postponing until some future period the direct effort to change adverse social matters, the Gospel bids each man who would "enter into life" to begin to act, live, think and love today as a member of the spiritual order, starting first with the power of the spirit to conquer the flesh.

We answer the question then, How does the spiritual science of Jesus differ from other sciences? by saying that it must be proved by each individual before he can prove it to another. In these four brief records called the Gospels are set down all the points needed to disclose the way to the perfect life for all who make effort to apply the Christ to the conditions at hand, shirking nothing, making no pretense, giving all to one Master. The way is narrow and strait, if you please,—and few are found entering upon it. So, too, the harvest is plenteous but the laborers few. In the case of those who turn aside there is a radical misunderstanding, namely, that one can obtain more happiness and greater freedom by going some other way. This is in very truth the way of the fulness of life which we all love whether we admit it or not. Each of us has the power to make the effort. The forces flowing hitherward from the divine centre are all tending that way. We were so constituted as to be able to walk in the way which the Master summoned us by setting the example. The true science of life is precisely this spiritual science of the Christ. There is no opposing power. The Gospel summons man to the perfect life. It summons him to freedom, health, happiness; therefore to fellowship with his brother man in this life of happiness, health and true freedom.

V

THE CHRIST METHOD

At first thought it seems too great a claim on our part to endeavor to heal by the method of Christ. For was not Jesus master of life and death, direct giver of life to men? Were not the works of healing different in kind from those wrought today? We find the Master speaking "with authority," not as men, but uttering decisive words which brought immediate consequence as by a miracle. Why then should we presume to accomplish works of a kindred nature?

Yet if Jesus's works of healing were wrought according to a science, this science becomes our standard and we can do no less than try to be faithful as far as the divine light has led us on our way. The Master does indeed speak with authority. He utters the affirmative words, "Be thou made clean," "Go thy way; as thou hast believed, so be it unto thee," "Stretch forth thine hand." It is our privilege, however, to consider how the affirmative word reaches the heart and sets the sufferer free. Jesus everywhere appeals to men to believe and follow. Attributing all the works of healing to the Father, he drew attention to those works as evidences of a principle which was known by its fruits. He promised other works to those believing on him, and taught that belief in him meant belief in God. Why should one do less than to take Jesus at his word, endeavoring faithfully to understand?

Comparison of the works of healing shows that Jesus proceeded according to a principle. Responding and appealing to faith, he healed when there was readiness to receive. This appealing attitude was so strong and outreaching that the centurion responded with implicit faith in behalf of his servant, not then present; the leper declared with full conviction, "Lord, if thou wilt, thou canst make me clean." One sufferer merely begged the privilege of touching the hem of Jesus's garment. Then, too, the Master repeatedly declared that he came to perform his works for "the lost sheep," he sent the disciples forth in quest of the lost and faithful, once more showing that works were to be wrought by a principle of intelligent response according to need. The disciples were not merely commissioned with power for special purposes, as if their works were to end by the withdrawing of that power. They were taught by precept and example in line with the whole Gospel as "the way, the truth, and the life." These instructions lose all their force if we try to confine them by the supposition that they implied special privileges.

Again, we find the Master displaying what seems like special knowledge of the hearts and minds of people around him, also knowledge of suffering people at a distance. He not only knows the thoughts of critics who hesitate to express their adverse sentiments, and the timid questionings of the disciples; but is able to tell the condition of the maid who was "not dead, but sleeping," and of Lazarus in successive stages of his sleep unto death. This discernment of the real in contrast with the apparent state was characteristic of his work among the sick as a whole. Surely this intuition was akin to that which we all possess in some degree, which some have had in marked degree who have recovered the method of spiritual healing, and which may be recognized and cultivated by all who believe in "the Christ within." To aspire to heal in this way is to make ready for that discernment which reveals the spiritual states of men and women ready for such healing.

Studying a given instance of healing, we note that Jesus took the clue from the affirmative attitude and its possibilities on the part of the sick or sorrowing. In the case of the man blind from his birth, Jesus explained that it was not that this man had sinned or that his parents were sinners. What he emphasized was the positive consideration, that is, the work of God which was made manifest through healing. The anointing with clay was incidental to this. The man when restored was true to the Master's confidence in him, as he courageously met the scepticism of the multitude. Presently the man went further and began to plead for recognition of the power of God, since no sinner could have wrought so marvellous a thing. "If this man were not of God, he could do nothing." Then Jesus met this display of faith with a further expression of confidence: "Dost thou believe on the Son of God?" The man did indeed believe, and he entered into the joys of his faith through acceptance of the Messiah. If this experience is in any way typical, we may see in it a verification of the science which the Master was teaching the disciples. Doubtless others responded in the same way through adopting the affirmative attitude.

The most touching incident, perhaps, is that of the woman taken in the act. Conventionally speaking there was every reason for condemnation. The Christians of the world at large have taken much the same position as that of the self-righteous men who gloried in their discovery of the woman. It is still customary to condemn, and to uphold a double standard of morality, instead of trying to discern the heart of both men and women with open vision. It was contrary to all expectations that Jesus should quietly occupy himself with drawing a figure upon the ground, then bid each guiltless critic cast a stone at the poor creature. The world has scarcely begun to make trial as yet of that higher resistance which left the Master alone with the accused — so persistently have we misunderstood what "non-resistance" means.

Connection having been broken with those forces which would have swept the guilty woman to her condemnation and made her an outcast for life, the Master turned in far-sighted charity to the accused. Jesus was not there to condemn. He took no account of conventional standards, or social appearances, but, as in all other instances of which we have record, looked deeply into the heart. For it was a question of the continued life of this woman, not of her mere past. She was a human spirit and had all the rights which any soul in need can ever have to be regarded as an individual, not as a mere unit in a social group belonging to a given nation. As a human spirit endowed with affection, she was summoned by the Master to come out into the light of her nobler self, to go and live for that self, the connection being broken with her sin. She was thus called toward the fulness of life because it was possible for her to respond. May we read in this an expression of that method which is universal either in disease or sin?

This faith in the human spirit did not mean neglect of actual circumstances under which the spirit meets experience. For on other occasions we find Jesus speaking plainly about dark spots in human society. He speaks of the good man and the evil man, according to the expressions they make of the life within. He refers to blind leaders of the blind, and warns his disciples regarding various forms of deceit. Throughout his teaching he shows that our words condemn or justify us, that every idle word brings its effect; hence that no man escapes from impurity of thought by any theoretic device meant to conceal or minimize. The Master in fact says plainly that his teaching comes to cause dissension, as a sword brings pain. Not in any way could he be said to compromise with destructive forces. Yet all his judgments are constructive. He comes to find lost sheep and call them home to that kingdom of love which every man may enter who will turn about and adopt the affirmative attitude. He comes that men may have life and have it more abundantly.

To be the Master's follower in the field of spiritual healing is to adopt as one's ideal this standard of spiritual health and see why people are held up to that standard. It would be impossible to emulate the Master without trying to live the Christian life in fulness, taking up the cross, losing one's life to find it, going and selling whatever riches one may have that stand in the way of loving Christ. He who would lead men as little children must himself become like those the Master blessed. He who would teach others how to forgive should begin by forgiving if he have aught against anyone. In short, he who would guide his fellow men into life is bidden first to "enter into life" himself. But all this is understood when we are speaking of any phase of Christian service whatever. There is but one law.

What we have so long failed to see is that the mode of life which the world has accepted as the ideal in a certain direction is the guide in all directions. That life, for example, is a life of giving, not "getting." It means acting unflinchingly by a higher principle, never resisting any force unfriendly to man on its own level but always on the upper level, through love. Healing in accordance with the Christ is an instance of this law of giving. Christ is the Giver of life. What all men need in their spiritual illnesses is this Life that quickens the heart, frees the spirit from its bondages. What all men need, Christ in the heart already knows. It is our human privilege to be a messenger of this gospel. If we have seen its truth in one sphere of human needs we realize that it applies equally to all. The world has not to any extent tried the principle of unstinted giving. So the world has not seen that this principle applies to healing.

In his sins and illnesses man shuts himself into a narrow world. He thinks and wills, schemes and acts for himself chiefly, considering how he can attain his private ends, how he may gain subtle sway over people, using them for his own interests. When pain and suffering and the consequences of his self-love come upon him man enters more deeply into self, asks to be freed from the results as mere results without inquiry into causes. A creature of outward things and interests for the time being, he expects to be set free by external forces. He professes to care nothing about what is spiritual. He simply wishes to go on with the game.

To be gifted with the Christ-spirit even in small degree is to see what is the trouble with man. To be touched more deeply by that spirit is to be moved with compassion. For man has separated himself in heart from his Maker. He is acting as if apart, detached from spiritual relationship with his brothers. The pains he suffers are meant to lead him to consciousness of his real situation. They are not hostile, not alien forces warring upon him, but blessings in disguise. But he is in a negative attitude, opposing the Love that would bless him, struggling not to see the lessons of experience. There will be no freedom for him while he rebels. But the Christ-love comes to him to lift him out of his rebellion that he may see what he is doing, may will to be free. It comes to give him back to himself. Therefore the discernment it brings makes the eye single to the ideal, inspires a vision of the self as made in the image and likeness of God, created to be in health and freedom.

The affirmative attitude on the part of the human spirit puts the soul of one who would serve as healer in touch with this outpouring or giving of Life. In the affirmative attitude we believe to the utmost and look for the highest. In that attitude we see the best in another and hold firmly to it. The efficiency is always from the one Giver of life, but this life becomes most active through us when we open the spirit to receive and give it as if it were our own. The affirmative is at the same time the giving attitude. In this attitude there is no condemnation, no judgment, no effort to influence another to go one's own way. There is full giving of oneself in service, that whatever is best for another may be spoken and may be done. To give is never merely to use, to control or manage. To give is to be ready to be used, to let the divine wisdom have full expression, to withhold nothing of the divine love.

Yet this unstinted giving of oneself that the spirit may be an unimpeded instrument of expression for the healing Christ, is not at random or merely in general. It is the essence of the Christ to incarnate itself, to unite the Word with the flesh in definite and concrete form. This is why in the example given us in the Gospels the Christ is always seen in relation to the most intimate needs of the individual, carrying purity into the thought, love into the heart, and a corresponding purification into the bodily life. Every individual is sacred to the Christ. There is comfort for every sorrowing heart. No man or woman, however separate in consciousness from recognition of this great wisdom, is too insignificant or even too sinful to warrant refusal to give. The one condition is willingness, faith, openness of heart such that the healing love may enter in.

Thus too every thought of ours, every mental ability to make our realization concrete, every prompting of the heart however slight may be dedicated to this divine service. There is every reason for asking for what we will "in the name of Christ," every reason for the prayer of the heart which believes that it will receive. "All things are yours" in that spirit. Now "we have the mind of Christ." We are renewed by that mind to utter the quickening word. And naturally in our prayers we will ask for more, since we now begin to realize at last something like the fulness of the promise, that other signs shall follow, that "greater works" will be done.

VI

SPIRITUAL HEALTH.

"If man had lived the life of good, his interiors would be open to heaven, and through heaven to the Lord; thus also the smallest and invisible vessels would be open, and man would be without disease." This statement admits us into the heart of the matter as spiritual health is regarded by one of our great seers. It tells us that man's rightful estate according to the divine purpose is one of health, happiness and freedom. There is an incoming life from our Creator tending to keep us in perfect health. Disease is not an infliction sent down upon us, suffering is not a means of discipline bestowed by a stern will, as devotees of a former theology used to say. Spiritually speaking, it is normal to be well and strong, and if normal to be in excellent health it is right for man to be free and happy. All our thinking in the matter should start from this the divine ideal, not from the negative fact of man's illnesses and sorrows. It follows that true spiritual healing comes about through an endeavor to return to our normal condition, that we need give attention to disease and its causes only that we may learn how to remove obstructions which impede the inflow of the divine life, the life which makes for our health and freedom.

To be prepared to see the force of this view of man's health we need to remind ourselves that real causes are spiritual, whatever else may also be true concerning life under natural conditions. Man is a spirit, and the source of his being is in God, in whom he lives, moves and has his being, from whom there comes the impetus to develop and achieve. The divine life enters his spirit from within, in "the heart" whence springs his inmost love and volition; and proceeds thence into his understanding, or the life of thought, and so on throughout his selfhood, into the physical organism. Openness of heart tends to illumination of the understanding, and an illumined understanding can express itself in a quickened brain, a harmonious nervous organism and physical system, if there be no hindrances not yet overcome. The centre of power is within the soul, in the first place, and the centre must be kept open and free if the currents of life shall have free opportunity to course through man's whole being. But the power received by man tends toward expression, to be as completely manifested as possible. There can be perfect correspondence between soul and body only so far as the life which touches the heart shall quicken every particle and possess every organ. For correspondence means the expression of spiritual power in exterior states. To be thoroughgoing it must be carried out into expression in every detail.

We are prepared then for another statement which touches the heart of the matter, namely, that "all diseases in man have correspondence with the spiritual world." This statement seems absurd at first, since we think of the spiritual world as "heaven." But the term is here used in its largest sense to include the entire realm of influences affecting the inner life of man. Heaven is order, harmony; but the power tending to produce it within us may be interfered with, and if there is selfishness or uncleanness at the centre there will be a corresponding outward expression. If the spiritual life sickens, if there is spiritual death, negation or strife, then the outward organism will manifest the conflict that is going on within. To say this is not to ignore any of the disturbances on the surface commonly called disease and attributed to purely physical causes. But these are secondary matters, and we are trying to look at the whole question in the light of what is primary.

If, for example, man is living a life of intemperance of any sort, there is both the effect produced on the body through drinking, smoking, excessive eating, inordinate physical desires and passions; and also the mode of life within man's selfhood which permits and fosters this intemperance, leading as it does from one excess to another. In contrast with all this excess, rational balance between tendencies and desires is health. If envy rules at the centre, if there is hate at the helm, revenge, anger, jealousy, bitterness, anxiety, worry; fear of the loss of money, reputation, or fear of punishment and death —in each case the person's life is affected according to the prevälence or persistence of the disordered state. Whatever evil desire, lust, or other selfish emotion arises to throw man's inner life into discord also causes the bodily organism to suffer. If man is in doubt, in inner strife or temptation, his mental and physical life respond accordingly. All these disordered states are traceable to the prevailing desire or love, since what man wants he pursues, and by putting forth his activity in the chosen direction he draws himself toward the conditions which fulfil his desire. We all know how the changes begin which cause our misery, if we are in the habit of noticing the immediate results in our feeling. To have an impulse to do a good act, to be charitable, forgiving, generous; and then to cut off this prompting to be generous by being mean, small, hateful, spiteful, is to find our inner life immediately narrowed, cramped, impeded.

Whatever removes man from tranquillity through worldly cares and anxieties, as quickly affects his outer life. When the inner life is unclean, the thoughts and emotions find ways of expression by enlarging upon this impurity. For our directions of mind readily grow into prevailing states and attitudes, fear and lust alike grow by what they feed upon. If there is mental weakness, a negative attitude, gnawing doubt, or despair; then this attitude affects our daily thought and conduct. But if the affirmative attitude prevails, if every incident is turned to account so as to give courage, to strengthen hope, lead to success, then equivalent outward results follow. To believe in success and to stick to this belief is indeed the sure way to secure an outwardly successful life.

The central consideration is never the effect or outward expression alone, however many attendant ills it may lead to; but the inward state from which it springs, the state which must be changed before the effects will change. "Since the causes of disease are in the spiritual world, and operate under the law of correspondences, and indeed are evils of that world, the diseases are not to be dreaded for what they are in themselves. The actual calamity or illness is in the spiritual evil it externally represents. It is selfishness which is the veritable thing to be dreaded. It is lust, jealousy, unkind thoughts, and enmities that are the real ill-health. Diseases of the body are material images of selfishness and sin. These are the concrete forms of our lusts. These mental things are their origin and their source of continuance."[1]

This is an unpleasant truth. People do not like to have their diseases connected with their life as a whole. They approve of the artificial separation which Christians have made for centuries between sin and sickness, in the face of the fact that Jesus identified the two and sought to establish spiritual health or wholeness. They wish to be cured of their illnesses as things apart, that is, as bodily maladies susceptible to physical remedies only, that they may go on gratifying their favorite desires as before. They wish to keep such intemperance or excess as may please them, according to the conventional life they lead; and they refuse to classify these excesses as sins or diseases. Nearly everybody objects to any sort of teaching, whether urged by the Church, by physicians, by science, or by social reformers of any school, however liberal or radical, which traces human ills and evils down to selfishness and bids man master himself. And

[1] "Psychiasis," C. H. Mann, pp. 128, 131.

so the would-be leaders and reformers are in league as it were not to make the indictment too severe. We do not like to be fundamental in our thinking. We do not like plain truths concerning our miseries. Too much effort would be required on our part were we to become free, sane and pure from the ground up, in all departments of life.

To say, however, that all diseases correspond with spiritual states is to realize that there are also spiritual states which mean freedom for us all. There is tranquillity, for example, serenity or peace at the centre with its equivalent ideas and emotions, calm and stable, and a well-ordered nervous system insuring inner control, skilful use of the brain and efficiency in outward work. There is interior openness to life, accompanied by what we call spontaneity of spirit, freshness of feeling, a certain youthfulness and vigorous power of accomplishment. When man acknowledges the one source of all life and power, and endeavors to live by the divine love and wisdom in all things, this responsiveness at the centre invites power which takes away any number of interferences within the self. There is obedience in the true sense, not through mere humility or any negative attitude, but through dynamic harmony with the divine will, the desire to be, to live and to act as God would have man act when attaining the fulness of life. Service is then the natural expression of the inner harmony. With faith at the centre there is adaptation to divine opportunities along the way. The moral life springs from the spiritual and man shows by his deeds in his home, in society, in civic service, in the commercial world, that he serves one master. To be a house at unity with itself is to be free from a thousand ills from which we find men suffering who have divided houses within them. In brief, it might be said that to be in disease or sin is to be trying to serve two masters; to be in health and freedom is to serve one Master, the Christ.

"He who lives in good," says Swedenborg, "and believes that the Lord governs the universe, and that all good is from the Lord alone, that all life is from Him, . . . thus that from Him we live, move, and have our being, is in such a state that he can be gifted with heavenly freedom, and together with it peace; for he then trusts solely in the Lord, and has no cares for other things, and is certain that all things are tending to his good, his blessedness and his happiness to eternity."[1] That is to say, man is thereby brought into a state of unity between his will and his understanding, he receives the divine influx *as one* and is at peace with God and man

[1] "Arcana Cœlestia," No. 2892.

in his spirit. He does not merely receive from within, he also gives. He does not seek first of all to get possessions or wealth, to acquire from his fellow men; he tries to give to men by performing his true function in the world as a constructive member of society. Since there is efflux or expression, there can be an ever greater influx from the divine source of love and wisdom.

It seems an enormous step from the external world where we are seeking the causes of diseases in unsanitary surroundings, in impure water and germs, to the realm of thought where health means spiritual unity within the self. In so far as man's environment is made sanitary and all obnoxious germs are destroyed, we expect man to be healthy, and all this without regard to what he may believe concerning spiritual things. But we have not been carrying on an equally vigorous campaign to teach man to appreciate and rightly use the sanitary environment we hope to create for him. We forget that health in the true sense includes every phase of man's life, and that when there is no inner understanding the forces of the external environment may count for naught. What we need above all is enlightenment expressing itself according to need in conformity with the spiritual standard.

Man cannot truly be understood in one part of his selfhood merely, as if he were a being of flesh and blood with an obscure entity called "the soul" somewhere hidden within the brain. To start with man in an adequate way is to begin with the great fact that he is spiritual and lives in both the spiritual world and the natural, partly recipient of spiritual forces within his spirit and partly associated with physical things and influences through his organism. The spiritual realm is in every conceivable sense the real domain of causes. Nothing in the natural world has any power of change, motion or life of its own; things in the natural world change, move and live by virtue of the immanent energies animating them, energies which exist for spiritual ends. This is true even when natural events appear to go contrary to order. The disorders of the natural world cannot be understood save through knowledge of the powers that normally make for order. Man being a spiritual being, living by spiritual influx, every event in his life must be put in relation to that central truth, however far removed it may seem from the ideal. If he suffers discords to break into the harmony of his life, these are due to misapplication of powers which are intended to produce harmony. There is but one efficiency in any event. The variations from harmony, health and freedom from which man suffers are one and all expressions of his own lack of adjustment to this one Life.

It becomes plain that the physical organism has no choice in what it shall express, since it is merely an instrument for the use of the spirit, obedient to the understanding and the will. Whatever the spirit wills, whatever man yields himself to as the goal of action, becomes manifest in bodily expression and conduct even though man permits himself to sink lower than the brutes. The body does not live from nature alone but from spirit. The body appears to move and live by itself because the spirit is in such intimate accordance with it that the two move as one. The spirit is within it in a connection as intimate as that of the fibre within the muscle. The spirit has in fact taken unto itself a body or visible form, it has clothed itself with the natural form as with a garment.

Since the physical organism is thus responsive to the spirit, it follows that when any disturbance such as anxiety, restlessness, ill-will, anger, jealousy, hatred, bitterness, malice or any other distemper that expresses selfishness becomes active or breaks forth within, then the brain responds, the nervous system also responds, and the physical organism as a whole reports the inner condition. This is true, whether it be merely a question of any angry emotion which shows itself in the flushed cheek, the clenched fist and the swift blow, or a question of deep-seated mental states steadily showing themselves in a life of habitual servitude to angry passions. There is disturbance whenever anger, hate, and the other disrupting emotions gain ascendency. This is so because man was made not for anger but for love, not for selfishness but for fellowship and service through response to the Fatherhood of God and the brotherhood of man. He was made for health, happiness and freedom. The life-energies should course through his being without let or hindrance. Whatever disturbs his inner life disturbs the life-currents generally. The more central the disturbance, the more wide-spread and serious are the effects coming from it. Whatever affects man's inner life affects his attitude toward the spiritual world and the energies coming therefrom; for man as a receptacle of life inevitably takes some sort of attitude, either by responsively adopting an experience, or by refusing and struggling against it. Thus any change of state within him affects his relationship to the divine life. Thus it is that really to explain his diseases however external they may seem, one must take into account what is at the same time in process at the centre, as he looks above and beyond himself in aspiration or as he looks more deeply within his lesser self in pettiness of motive. In either case he turns in a certain direction of mind which carries with it a sphere of influences. For all his states have their likenesses in the forces which they attract and to which they correspond.

To say this is not to declare that the influence of the spirit upon the body is the only influence that results from man's disordered inner life. The physical organism as we well know is not like a channel through which a stream flows one way only, it is not like an utterly silent servant or mere machine. The soul influences the body and in the course of time makes manifest whatever is in process inside, marking in the face the results of anxiety, nervousness, inner conflict, repression, unhappiness, domestic troubles; or touching it with evidences of beauty and serenity of character, as the case may be. But the body also stores away for future trouble or future harmony the states into which it has been shaped by long-continued activity, by habit, misuse, excess, indulgence. These adverse physical conditions act in the course of time like counterforces to impede and deaden the spirit. If the inner life is constrained, distraught, rebellious, cantankerous, the body faithfully shows the consequences and sends them back upon the soul. Thus the conservative, crystallized, deadened inner life of the person who adheres to an old system of belief with rigid aristocracy and arbitrary intolerance becomes manifest in conditions of the physical system that in turn still further deaden the inner life.

The various stages are seen in the case of unclean desires of various sorts. These spring in the first place out of misuse of instinctive forces in themselves wholly good. The excesses in due time quicken desires which grow by what they feed upon, and lead to further indulgence. If man yields he goes over to the side of selfishness. His nervous system and bodily organism obediently carry out and foster his desire, giving it back with increase. Thus the body comes in time to condition the mind. To the extent that this condition increases man becomes the creature of the instrument he should have controlled. When such a condition results, something more radical than a change of mind must occur. The body must be cleansed. Some spiritual influence must touch and transform the man, that he may take possession of his instrument, and make it alive with spiritual health. Only through a transformation of both spirit and body can he become "every whit whole." It is the power of the divine Spirit within him, the healing Christ which accomplishes this wondrous work.

VII

SPIRIT AND BODY

In the endeavor to learn just how the spirit controls the body, it is important to note that man may either give assent to bodily tendencies or refrain from such desires. Thus he may be either slave or master, in the one case apparently without any control over his body at all, in the other with every evidence of such control. Whichever way he turns, and whether seeming to control his body or not, his assent or endeavor to control becomes an attitude which gathers its like and influences the body, an attitude which continues to be effective in that way until checked by a stronger activity than that of the tendency in question.

The body is adapted to receive the living forces which flow in from the spirit in such a way that man may act spontaneously, scarcely aware that his bodily organism conditions his spiritual life. But inasmuch as spirit and body act as one, whatever interferes at one point interferes more or less in all; for example, when a toothache or some other pain localized in a small region upsets the customary activities of daily life as a whole. Hence it comes about that the spirit feels the weight of bodily interference and seems to have no power to withstand the obstacles or enticements of the flesh. To learn that the spirit possesses entire control and impels the body to do whatever it does is to become aware of the activities by which the spirit has unwittingly permitted divine forces making for health and purity to be interfered with.

If the inner life is in a state of rebellion, distraught by anxieties and tensions, the spirit by yielding to these states and permitting them to increase thereby gives assent to their expression in the body, with all the consequences that may ensue. In a sense man still rules his flesh even when given over to the greatest lusts, for the flesh always obediently portrays man's feelings and carries out his desires. This subservience will continue as long as man so wills. The source of evil is not in the flesh, as the mediæval Christians thought. There is no reason to mortify the flesh. We make no headway while we attribute either the trouble or the efficiency to the body. To do this is to be submissively a prisoner of the flesh. Nor do we make progress while we conciliate and indulge the body, on the ground that the flesh is strong and the spirit weak. One could not ask for more faithful servants than these remarkably responsive bodies of ours, adapted as they are to the slightest change of attitude on our part. There is plainly a great difference between a life of self-gratification and one of self-control. Yet, strange as it may seem, either condition reveals the supremacy of the spirit. Control at the centre means control all through, and sometimes mere assent to a bodily desire is the equivalent of control. The same power which weakly submits would suffice to give man a strong hold in the beginnings of self-mastery.

To adopt this deeper clue to the relationship of the spirit and body is not to advocate the short and easy road to health advertised by those who regard "wrong thoughts" as the only causes of disease. For a man might mend his thoughts in part and still give his will over to evil desires in other respects, or he might indulge in idealistic affirmations in one direction without endeavoring to change his bodily life in conformity thereto. Man is not essentially an assemblage of thoughts, despite the fact that in large measure he tends to make of himself what he thinks and by giving himself to directions of mind experiences the consequences of his own mental acts. He is more truly a will, a centre of desires and affection, with a prevailing love. It is this dominant desire which gives direction to his thoughts. He is influenced most by that which he steadily wills to be. If you can touch him at heart so that he is willing to turn from his old mode of life, opening his whole nature to receive the powers that make for goodness and health, then indeed his thoughts will conform, his mental imagery will be called into play, his emotions will correspond, and his external life will begin to show signs of change. So in the case of the nervous person, the creature of tensions and anxieties, there is no radical cure save through a spiritual process which reaches the centre, induces a fundamental change through cultivation of the life which leads to nerve-control and moderate well-balanced outward deeds.

To attain health and freedom one may well bestow the usual care upon the body, attending to its nourishment according to the most approved ideas, giving it abundant exercise, observing the conditions which men in their prudence have discovered. Indeed, one who is seeking health by spiritual means would naturally go farther than this, noting in detail those physical conditions which most favor the spirit in the effort to regain full sanity and control. One would expect the spiritual idealist to undergo a change of tastes, steadily bringing the physical life up to the standard. Some of these results would come about spontaneously, and a man would find himself no longer caring for luxuries and means of gratification which formerly expressed his servitude.

Yet the involuntary consequences are not always enough. Some must work and co-operate from the outside as faithfully as possible to make the physical organism a more fitting vehicle of expression. Many of us are so external, so little aware of the inner life, that we can best adopt the appropriate inner attitude if we first make an external change, just as one feels stronger in mind by standing erect in a position which suggests and commands strength. To begin in this way is not necessarily to put emphasis upon external things, is not to yield one's powers of thought or will. One may begin at either end and work toward the other. In any event one makes such changes for the benefit of the spirit, that the whole life may correspond with the spiritual ideal. To co-operate from without by breathing deeply, taking exercises, and eating pure food, is to open the organism for receiving the inflow of spiritual life from within.

There is in fact no reason for making light of the laws and conditions of natural healing, for the divine ideal coincides with these. All healing in the sense of the restoration of function or wasted tissue has a natural basis. In so far as the organism is restored the spirit has free expression. The spirit, by overcoming fear, anxiety, exciting emotions, haunting mental pictures and weak attitudes, removes the inner resistances to these natural restorative processes. The resistances overcome, the next step is the substitution of attitudes which actively co-operate with powers making for health. Such co-operation means opening the way for free passage of life from within outward. There is a sense in which all power resides in the external form, that is, when life has this freedom to course through to the extremities so that the natural garment may perfectly express the spirit. The increasing health of the organism ought to be the regular accomplishment of man's growth in spiritual things. Perfect health would thus be perfect expression of an inner life according to the spiritual order.

It is not primarily a question of supremacy over the flesh as if the body contained nothing friendly to the spirit. The body contains nothing unfriendly save what man himself has generated in it. It needs regeneration with man's own spiritual rebirth. It needs to be purified with the purification that is thorough. To try to make out that it is pure while neglecting to purify the spirit would be absurd. To ignore it as if it were unreal is to make ready for more trouble. Its true reality is the rightful privilege of the servant carrying out the behests of its master. Every instinct, function, organ, is good in its proper place; and all its organs and functions are for man's health and freedom.

True health for the body, in contrast with either physical methods which reach part way or mental alleviations which promise freedom through "demonstrating over" the body, depends upon recognition of the source of power and reality in the body. Since the interiors of the body make one or act as one with the interiors of the mind, when those of the mind are turned toward the divine source of power those of the body turn in like manner. Thus to turn in spirit toward the sources is to begin to regain the pristine condition of openness which means perfect health. The more truly we understand this law of inner turning and outer response, the less attention we need give to the details of the process. It will then be a question of lifting the spirit more and more into unison with the divine Spirit, that harmony may increase from more to more.

As one writer puts it, "No living thing has life apart from God. All life is an influx from Him who is life itself; it is variously manifested in different living things because of the difference in the forms into which it is received. Man's life is conveyed primarily to the soul and through it to the body, which has the appearance of life only while the spirit dwells in it. Perfect health results when the inflowing life from the Lord is received fully and freely. This is possible only when His laws are observed on both the natural and the spiritual planes. . . . Even more essential than care of the body on the natural plane is the observance of the laws of God on the spiritual plane. Since life flows into the body through the soul, the body can receive a full normal influx only when the life of the soul is in accordance with spiritual laws. Even the people who do not understand this truth recognize the tremendous influence which the mental state exerts upon the bodily condition and emphasize the importance of encouraging only kind and elevating thoughts and of cultivating a serene spirit."

It has also been pointed out by those who understand this truth in part that "physical health does not necessarily prove the presence of spiritual health nor physical ill-health the lack of it." That is to say, man's external life receives influences from the external world, and his physical condition may differ greatly from his spiritual state. Hence it happens that people who are almost devoid of spirituality are in robust health while others who are spiritual have frail or diseased bodies. Many have been mystified by this break in the correspondence between inner and outer conditions. It has been pointed out by some that the individual in ill-health is not always directly responsible. He may not personally have been guilty of the transgression of laws by which his condition has been brought about, but may be suffering from acts of his parents and of the society in which he lives through failure to provide pure water, sanitation and food inspection, and to guard against epidemics and pestilences. Some one else has pointed out that therefore "sick people are not morally responsible for their diseases; if they were, sinners would always be ill and saints would always be well; and human freedom would be lost, for no one could do wrong nor think falsity without immediately suffering physical harm as a result, and he could not proceed far in evil courses without meeting an early end in physical death."

Strangely enough, however, this qualification is so urged that the value of the idea of spiritual healing is wholly lost, and there is no resource left save to depend solely upon medical treatment in the conventional way. It is argued, for example, that since there are two distinct worlds, the natural and the spiritual, each with its sources of power, the body receives life or energy from the one, the spirit from the other; and there are natural laws governing the life of the body, spiritual laws for the spirit. "Obedience to the former . . . gives the body harmony with its environment, or physical health. Therefore saints and sinners are alike benefited by the shining of the sun on earth, and may share together the blessings or the curses of natural law. . . . Thus bodily conditions are the basis of health and disease, in common with all material conditions as a basis of earthly blessings or hardships."

To adopt this view literally would be to draw such distinctions between the natural world and the spiritual that we would completely lose sight of the great idea of the dynamic, life-giving influx from God. This view also ignores the fact that more depends upon the spirit's way of taking the conditions of life than on those conditions. We are indeed subject to external influences directly affecting the body. We are also subject to social influences without number, to the "mental atmospheres," the crowd-spirit, to suggestion, to waves of mental influence. Psychical influences also affect us. There are spheres on spheres of influence. But the modern devotee of spiritual healing assures us that the primary consideration is the sphere of influences to which we become open: all depends upon the point of contact, and the attitude adopted. Thus an undesirable inheritance tending toward disease is an opportunity to test our mettle. Back of the inheritance is the disposition or temperament. Possibly the entire environment, favorable or unfavorable, is for the testing of the spirit.

However dependent the body may be upon natural forces, its equilibrium is readily upset by fear, the nervous system becomes weak and tremulous, the normal rhythms of the heart and lungs are interfered with, and it has even been said that toxins are generated in the tissues, devitalizing the blood for body-building. More significant still, the equilibrium is rapidly restored when fear and other exciting emotions are overcome through the regaining of inner control and an affirmative attitude. The worst of all emotions is hate. It has been said that if a person could hate intensely and steadily for one hour, exhaustion or death would ensue. Contrariwise, the most helpful of all emotions is love, and love alone has sufficed to save the lives of both children and adults. What we are concerned with is those spiritual states which, while co-operating with the natural restorative forces of the body at their best, also open the spirit to the more direct incoming of divine power.

We note, too, that while sinners, also athletes and others in perfect physical health, may be as open as anyone to natural forces such as sunlight, when illnesses come like dread spectres from the outside world there is no power of inner resistance and a man's apparently splendid health counts for naught. On the other hand, a person with a frail physique but with spiritual understanding which he applies and spiritual power which he uses, may stem a tide which would sweep a physically strong man down to death. Thus the man who is apparently weakest and most severely handicapped by his "unfortunate inheritance," may through self-knowledge and mastery over his organism develop very great power in meeting conditions tending to produce disease. Far more important than external conditions, whatever they may be, is a man's way of meeting them.

To dwell upon the adverse external conditions and one's servitude to them would be to find the mind overwhelmed and apparently helpless. But those who have proved the power of the spirit over the body have practically ignored the secondary conditions of disease, discounting even the fact of inheritance, and have faced what was before them with positive determination to conquer. The results they have achieved lead one to believe that the primary consideration is always the spirit's way of taking life.

One person will submissively yield to a physical illness, or an injury due to a fall or broken bone, taking immediately to his bed and lying there as if his attitude in the matter had nothing whatever to do with the physical condition. Thus he will yield his body completely, without knowing that he is submitting it. But another person, while observing all the conditions that are prudent, so that the injured member may be put in order and be healed, will in every way cooperate with nature in spirit and be up and about the first moment his victorious spirit will permit. Another will go further still and actively cooperate in spirit because of knowledge of his true estate as a spiritual being open to divine life from within.

The virtuous man will have a great advantage on account of the purity of his life. It is a moral privilege to be well, and true moral obedience is of the inner life. The so-called saint may lack the faintest conception of the divine influx as an immediate resource in times of every sort of trouble. The saint makes a virtue of a few activities only, ignoring the law of expression through the external life as true evidence of inner harmony. Some saints also make a virtue of resignation to bodily ills, as if God preferred to have us suffer in a meek spirit. The so-called sinner may have advanced much further in real victory over hypocrisy, may have a control over the bodily organism which might well cause the saint to become envious. These matters can never be understood, therefore, by observation of the body alone, nor by study of the influences and conditions by which it is environed. What we must know in order to understand the law is *the state of the spirit,* its measure of control, its actual development, its openness to life. Restraint, discipline, is not necessarily a virtue; nor are all men sinners who possess freedom of expression, spontaneity or obedience to life. All these matters must be reassessed in the light of the spiritual standard of health.

VIII

TRUE SPIRITUAL HEALING

HEALING in the spiritual sense of the word begins with the discovery of our inner powers as children of God, made in His image and likeness. For through such discovery we learn that the spirit is potentially a master and can overcome interior and far-reaching causes of human misery. From this time forth it is never a mere question of illnesses and external obstacles to be surmounted, but of the attitudes, beliefs, habits, which underlie external conditions and give them their power over us. Instead of combating errors or denying the power of fears, it is a question of cultivating the affirmative spiritual states which make for freedom and happiness: faith, good-will toward all, charity, loyalty.

To "repent," that is, turn about and away from our troublesome desires in pursuit of their diviner opposites, is one step; to press forward despite all discouragements and conflicts, is another and usually a much harder one. For this involves a series of changes deeper in nature than any mere thinking about ideals. It means earnest desire to have the whole selfhood with its diverse promptings and interests made profoundly one. In this progress toward the deeper unity or integrity of the self man reaches a point where he can no longer divide his nature and seek to ward off certain consequences only, trying to escape from the necessity of coming to judgment in other respects. He can no longer dictate terms. If he really desires freedom he must observe laws and conditions with which he has nothing to do save to obey. For man's true freedom is found, not through discovering ways of his own, but in choosing and moving with the guidances which lead into the divine way. Man does not create the alternatives which life offers, the opportunity to look up or down, in or out; to move with the constructive powers or against them; to be affirmative or negative. Yet he has remarkable power over life through his will to turn in the one way or the other, to change to the affirmativc attitudc.

When man is ready to see this real situation in life, as he is held in equilibrium between opposing forces, looking with open eye courageously into his spiritual past and with hope into his spiritual future, then indeed he may be healed with that healing which means complete sanity. Severe and rigid seem to be the conditions which hold him to his task, binding him to a present in which he reaps the consequences of his unthinking past and the failures of his ancestors. Yet the same power which long appears to be his enemy, standing over him like a slave-driver, proves to be the God of infinite love whose disguised blessings begin at last to be understood. Man begins to be free and to find that the power that appeared to be hate was love, when he becomes enlightened about the opportunities which life offers him, when he chooses opportunities that are constructive.

It does not suffice, one insists, to specialize on those matters commonly regarded under the head of "sin," leaving man's health to be considered by other specialists. Ill-health of any sort is no less truly a sin or failure to achieve the type. For all phases of man's life move forward together, sin and sickness are sufficiently akin to touch the whole individual: the healing which "saves" must rescue the entire man and lead him into the fulness of life.

Whenever any one has marked off man's sinful nature in a sphere by itself as indicative of the hell man is making for himself, leaving him to repent by reckoning with his sins as if those were isolated matters, there has been a tendency to acquire self-righteousness, as if one were better than other people. But when one sees that all these matters belong together, there is no resource left save through healing for all. There is no longer even a theoretical stopping-point in the discrimination between God and man, the spiritual world and the natural, as if doctrinal distinctions were virtues. If the idea of the divine influx of love and wisdom means anything at all, one sees that man's proper relation to it is *dynamic throughout every portion of his being,* that man is so constituted as to receive and appropriate the influent life in the plentitude of many-sided health.

Our view of human nature is different from the beginning, when this becomes the ideal. We start with the inspiriting idea that man is by nature a highly organized spiritual being, adapted to receive and appropriate influent divine life in minuteness of detail, giving it freedom to pass into wise expression with creative efficiency. We give up the notion that his spirit is a filmy essence vaguely filling the body or timidly inhabiting the brain. We give our thought entire liberty to develop to the full this ideal of the spirit as master-life, master-substance underlying and strengthening the body according to need. We then think of each little receptacle as being brought into orderly relation and response, that the whole body may become in actuality what it is ideally from the beginning, "the temple of the Holy Spirit." Giving our thought to this glorious conception more and more, we may follow out very intimately and fully the idea that there flows into the soul a life which should touch every portion of our being. Realizing in spirit the vital reality of this inflow, then experiencing it as a quickening result throughout the organism, we may give thought to the needs of our brother man, exemplifying what we mean by the divine influx as a life, not a mere theory; a healing power, not a mere summons to forego certain of our sins; a love guiding us to spiritual service, not a mere feeling to give us consolation that we are "saved."

The soul thus environed by divine possibilities has been graphically compared to a tree out in the sunlight receiving from the sun's warm and vitalizing rays what is essential to its perfect growth. Without the incoming energy from the sun, the tree has no life, despite the richness of the soil. In response to this descending energy, the tree passes through remarkable stages of assimilation, through changes wrought within the structure by the life that enters every cell. Enlarging upon the comparison and recollecting that man develops instruments of receptivity and expression by use, we have a vision of the human spirit bathed in the warm, soft light of the Spirit, touched in "the secret place" of the heart by descending love and wisdom. What sort of practical realization or service is worthy of this sublime relationship? What truth is more widely needed than this, namely, that here at hand, in the vital hour of interest and need, the soul may enter in and receive from a source as bountiful as that from which the tree draws sustenance but many times increased, and of a quality infinitely higher?

According to Swedenborg's statement of this vital relationship, there is an influx into the soul of each one of us at all times, in every moment, otherwise we could not exist and would not survive; an influx which not only sustains us but protects and guides us, withholding man by a "very strong force" from influences which tend to his injury. That is to say, this heavenly or divine influx really "rules every one" whatever the appearances to the contrary and despite man's failure to give recognition to it. This it is that keeps man's life within bounds, drawing him into the pathways of his progress in loving protection and care. It rules man "not in the universal, but in the veriest singulars," in the smallest things of life; it is the divine providence which is equal to every emergency. Although we are generally speaking unaware of this influx, so wrapped up in our own concerns that we may even ignore and oppose it, the divine life comes "in so vivid a manner" that man can notice it. For man already contains the powers which would make it possible for him to live with open vision toward the source of his life, with intimate knowledge of the favorable and unfavorable forces that play upon him.

While few of us may have been so illumined and quickened as to become vividly aware of this influx, able to distinguish by actual perception between life coming from the spiritual world, in contrast with influences coming from the natural world through the body or from the minds of people round about us, every one may attain an ideal of this conscious relationship with the divine presence by noting the elements of it and letting them grow into a clear idea.

First, in regard to health, note that from this point of view it is not physical health or even moral health which should be sought as the end. For if health is sought for itself aside from the spiritual life we may depart from the divine order, which is by growth from within outward, from spiritual things to natural. We might then mistake for ends in themselves activities which should be co-operative, such as the endeavor to keep the body well exercised and in prime condition, the use of pure foods, and the like. What one should seek is the permanent inner state of freedom, peace, tranquillity, from which health will spring as a ready consequence if we are living a divinely useful life. One seeks this end by working first and last for the spiritual type of life in human society. One realizes that the very import of this interior influx is that it shall bring precisely this health which does not stop short of true service according to our fullest ability. One emphasizes the realization by making the ideal as vivid as possible, making it an uplifting picture of that which is to be.

Inasmuch as the influent life first touches the affectional nature or "heart" in the secret place, one thinks of divine love as entering in with quickening power to establish the right balance in intellectual things. Love in this creative sense is simply unspeakable. Yet intuitively we all know that it can accomplish the great miracle within us. We think of this life as reaching into the understanding, touching it into illuminating thought; and thence affecting the whole mind, the nervous organism and the body, accomplishing its work wherever needed. Inasmuch as all power is in this influx, as it tends outward to that which is most external in thc body, one thinks of it as meeting and overcoming obstructions, lessening tensions, carrying out impurities. Once more one sees the importance of any co-operation from without which tends to keep the organism open and free—just as when inwardly intense we draw deep breaths, relax, and otherwise regain the normal rhythms while interiorly yielding up our tensions.

This realization of the divine influx becomes

most effective when one sits down in a quiet place alone, or with someone who needs help. One seeks the divine wisdom by closing the door upon the outer world and opening the inner window that looks upon the spiritual world. We attain a similar attitude in prayer for the sake of worship when prayer is really effective; for in true prayer there is an upliftment of heart and will, an opening out to receive with the conviction that it is man, not God, who needs to change. True prayer, the Gospels tell us, is to the Father who already knows what needs we have and has provided for them through the orderly incoming of life. If to such a prayer one adds the realization that the Father is as surely present as of old, present in all detail and minuteness, in the relation of Heart to heart, through the divine in the human, one may make the prayer as vivid as the experience which the spiritual healer calls "realization."

In a realization of the divine presence for immediate spiritual benefit one needs to forget distinctions which are pleasing to doctrinal people, and to transcend all barriers in quietly deep desire to let the divine life enter without let or hindrance. For the time being one thinks only of divine relationships, remembering that man is made in the image and likeness of God. Thus while frankly acknowledging what one has learned from mistakes, one no longer identifies the true self with the self that thus erred. For whatever the evidences that man acts as if of himself, as a separated self subject to adverse influences, in self-love and love of the world, one refuses for the moment to think in those terms: *one thinks of man now in his larger estate.* In that larger estate it is God who achieves, not man. It is the divine life in us that leads us to freedom and productiveness. Man has no power in and of himself to work such wonders. The power which man appears to have in sheer independence is due to an apparent cutting off of himself as if he were his very own, an isolated unit seeking private ends in disregard of God and man. In very truth man is never cut off. He lives from God. He enjoys freedom through the divine presence. God is the real source of health and strength. Unceasingly man is sustained by life from the spiritual world.

This realization is strengthened by the thought that all power is in spiritual life, and that there is no rival power. That is, the soul is a spiritual being constituted of spiritual substance organized for the freer life in the spiritual world that is to come as well as for experience in this world. The spirit has ruling and conquering power over the flesh. It can transcend physical conditions and become active on the higher level. Every thought is a help that is affirmative. Thought by thought one can build up a habit, an attitude that is favorable to the spiritual will. It is will or love which accomplishes the greater work.

Again, there is strength and helpfulness in the realization that to co-operate with the divine the human will needs to make affirmative effort. This is important for those inclined to yield too much or carry self-sacrifice to the extreme. If our attitude becomes weak we may be as far from true adjustment to the divine life as people who assert the self autocratically. Half the art of the spiritual life, so far as the individual regarded by himself is concerned, consists in knowing how far to go in our endeavor to claim the place which belongs to us. Each must learn this lesson from experience, as a part of the larger lesson which our whole inner life is intended to teach.

Can one benefit another by the kind of realization which brings spiritual healing for oneself? Certainly, since we are intimately "members one of another" in the inner world. It is a question of substituting nobler influences for those which we already exert. The world of thought which we enter is essentially a social world, despite the fact that we seem to be more alone when we meditate. There we are connected by spiritual ties with those akin to us and those whom we can help. We live more intimately with these our real affinities than we ever suspect. We can learn to put ourselves more fully in line with the divine incoming life through which there are greater opportunities for helpfulness than in anything external. The true test of relationship to the divine influx is not in mere receptivity or meditation for our own benefit, but in helping others into freedom.

The spirit of man, let us remind ourselves, is essentially dynamic, a user of power rightfully supreme over thoughts and emotions, instincts and desires; it rightfully controls the flesh. One who truly understands the connection between the spirit and the flesh, instead of ignoring the body, should be able to gain a control over it impossible from the point of view of merely mental healing. For he should be able to overcome every obstacle in his nature which impedes the inflow of the divine life. This would mean active co-operation with that life all along the line of existence, spiritually, morally, socially, physically, in accordance with one standard.

Thus we start in every instance with the same great idea, namely, that man is a spirit dwelling interiorly in a world of higher power, the home of the Spirit within the human heart. In that world it is not a question of space but of interior states and their expression. The human spirit is not separated from fellow spirits, but is drawn nearer those akin by every accordant act. To desire to be like another whose attitude and conduct are more nobly spiritual, is to put oneself nearer the source of the other's power. To desire to help another is to be with him in spirit, adding one's might in favor of the best that is in him, seeing him in spirit from the viewpoint of the ideal. To make even a little headway in such service is to realize that one must become a more fitting instrument of the infinite life.

Once succeed, therefore, in transferring your centre of thought from the physical world, as if you were a thing of flesh and blood, bound down by physical forces and forms, and a new world of realities opens before you. Point by point your thought may be brought round to correspond. Begin to look outward, in touch with the outgoing stream from the inner life into the body, then the rest will follow. For you will see that, as you once impeded the courses of life streaming through you by endeavoring to stem the tide no man can turn, so now your possibilities of co-operating are without limit. The interferences you offered in your ignorance, your folly, pride, impatience, self-conceit, arrogance and selfishness, wrought misery enough for yourself and those associated with you; but they did not really change you as a person or alter the course of life. You begin to be healed from the moment you see the sources of trouble in yourself, your attitude and the mode of conduct springing from it; for you then cease to blame your neighbors and your God, and begin with yourself. Your restoration will continue in so far as you transfer your allegiance to the ever-present, inflowing life which never seeks anything within you short of your freedom, your health, your larger social service. In so far as you become sane at the centre, you may become an instrument for that wise sanity which the divine providence is ever ready to reveal.

IX

THE AFFIRMATIVE ATTITUDE

LORD, I believe; help thou mine unbelief.—Mark ix, 24.

Without question, most of us who are endeavoring to live the spiritual life, frequently find ourselves in the state of spirit indicated above. "Jesus said unto him, If thou canst believe, all things are possible to him that believeth. And straightway the father of the child cried out, and said with tears, Lord, I believe; help thou mine unbelief." We see clearly that without childlikeness of heart, no one may enter the heavenly life. In our desire to maintain the right kind of simplicity of spirit and of life, we often look back to a period in the life of the soul expressed by the fidelity of young Samuel, when in entire responsiveness of heart he said, "Here am I. . . . Speak, Lord; for thy servant heareth." Inasmuch as the natural man is strongly self-assertive, we wish to avoid any claims in our own behalf, that we may learn to walk in the way of the Lord. Therefore we ask, "What wilt thou have me to do?" Again, we are taught that there is but one source of life or power, that man is a recipient of the Divine Love and Wisdom. As instruments of life, we wish to be true in every way to the heavenly standard. We realize that "all things are possible to him that believeth," but the question is, How may we acquire the right attitude without making too much of ourselves?

It requires little observation, however, to discover that as some men err in self-assertiveness, so others overdo in their endeavors to be receptive. Our belief concerning man as a receptacle of life often leaves us in a state akin to passivity, as if our part were merely to receive and retain. Inasmuch as no man can serve two masters, he who is not actively working to serve the cause of righteousness may be virtually against that cause, like the pacifist in war time who merely stands apart in protest. "He that is not with me is against me; and he that gathereth not with me scattereth." So-called passive obedience is not true responsiveness. What is demanded of us is not merely recognition but co-operation. They really stand for and serve the kingdom who actively put themselves in line with work that is in progress. No half-way measures suffice. We are bidden to serve with all our might, just as we are bidden to "love the Lord thy God with all thy heart, and with all thy soul, and with all thy mind, and with all thy strength." This is very emphatic language. He who is trying in every way to be true to this commandment, earnestly desires to know what kind of social activity should spring from true interior receptivity. For he wishes to be a man in full spiritual right.

A direct clue to the affirmative attitude is found when we regard it in the light of victory over temptation. The negative attitude is due in part at least, to doubt or hesitancy. Naturally those who wish to tempt us do whatever is in their power to keep us in a state of suspense. Thus dark influences have access to us. On the other hand, the power of the good with us tends to dispel doubt, hence to overcome the negative attitude, that the door may be closed to all undesirable influences. While in temptation, man hangs between the negative and the affirmative. To become actively responsive to the divine life, we must be strong in our hope, firm in faith, that we may be helped into a spiritual state, in which we are habitually in the affirmative. In war time we saw the importance of the affirmative attitude. We declared with entire conviction that the right would win, that it must win. We could not afford to doubt.

"Assurance respecting the result precedes the victory and belongs to the victory." This assurance bespeaks the moral attitude. By holding to what we believe to be the right with strong conviction, we launch our energies with carrying power, we call our reserves into play. As matters go in the world, we need some great incentive, we need to face a crisis or disaster in order to be called into fulness of action and show what we are able to accomplish. Only by adopting the affirmative attitude in full strength, is man able to depend on the powers of the moral order to the full. The man who thus acts is not active in his own might. Although apparently acting as if all power were his own, he is in reality co-operating with the divine will.

Again, we note the power of the affirmative attitude when it is a question of spiritual truth. We may not as yet be able to grasp a principle as true. We may desire to accept it, but objections may arise. If, however, we are willing to make the venture on faith, noting the practical results, it may forthwith become a truth to us. Our teachings far surpass our power of present verification, but we can at least be affirmative in regard to them. If we hold to a principle because we believe it is divine, this fidelity will bring its reward in the shape of sure convictions. It is the affirmative attitude which quickens us to gain spiritual wisdom. By wisdom in contrast with mere knowledge, we mean truth that has borne the test, knowledge we have dared to live by. It comes forth from our lips with the power of life behind it. We have ventured to stand by it and it has stood by us. Seldom do we grow in spiritual truth without an act of faith. And faith is an efficient, constructive power in the spiritual life.

The affirmation of spiritual truth "that it is so" because of the source from which it came, is indeed the beginning of the mind's regeneration. By taking this step, even when we cannot see clearly, we ally ourselves with the constructive powers. The human part consists in making the venture. Only when thus left free to choose and to venture, could we be morally free. Our human situation often seems uncertain. So indeed it is while we waver between the negative and the affirmative. Yet a slight effort may turn the scale. Even in our uncertainty we may test the great promises. To cry out in our uncertainty, "Lord, I believe; help thou mine unbelief," is to change from weakness to strength. Much depends on willingness to cast the die. The result is a new centre of equilibrium.

We hardly need to be told that "the good cannot flow into what is negative." The good, we know, comes to us to accomplish results, to operate through us. It is with us to flow from the inmost to the outmost, to take form in practical service enlisting our social nature. Granted the expression of what has come, although it be a mere beginning in the life of charity, more can be added. While our minds dwell upon the abstract or general principle, we still belong with people classified as negative. We often meet people who are in a vague intellectual state. There is much scattering of force among those who try to believe so many things, those who are merely liberal, broad-minded; hence indefinite. "He that is not with me is against me; and he that gathereth not with me scattereth." To be affirmative is to come out into the open, to take sides, show our loyalty, speak out. It is to adapt ourselves to our age at a promising point, where activities are in process and people are testing out what they believe.

We often look with a feeling akin to envy on people who are cultivating their powers with no thought for the time being save for self-expression. There seems to be an advantage in this form of concentration. No energy is lost in self-disparagement. There is no effort to be self-sacrificing. There is expression, life, energy. In contrast with this free self-development, people who are trying to be good Christians frequently lose headway by undue self-examination, by the effort to be duly humble, contrite. The highly conscientious person may spend most of his energies trying to learn in advance precisely what he ought to do. Others discount every talent they possess in their zeal to overcome the self. Christian self-sacrifice, as many pursue it, is chiefly negative.

Yet why should we discount the self in this way? Is there any real conflict between the cultivation of our talents to the full and their use for divine ends? What more could God ask of us than that we should be productive individuals, expressing character to the utmost? For no one can endeavor to express himself to the full without considering what he can do best in the world, what he can contribute to society as it exists today, how he may best realize a definite purpose. Man in deepest truth is "an organ of life." He cannot underestimate the prompting to come forth and live out his life to the full without disparaging his Creator. Self-sacrifice is not the end; dedication to a purpose, devotion to an ideal, is the standard. Devotion is a positive term. It is affirmative.

The older theology was nearly always negative in emphasis. It dwelt overmuch on the sinfulness of man, the depravity of human nature, and the weakness of the flesh. It painted the world in dark, lurid colors, and had more to say about hell than about heaven. It condemned the world and found fault with even the simple natural pursuits. It dwelt on the sufferings of the cross, the atoning blood, the sacrificial death, as if the race were to be saved by these negative considerations. It emphasized the resurrection instead of the glorification and the saving life that went forth into the world. The human self was supposed to emulate the Saviour in all these negative ways. The goal was escape from the woes of the flesh through mere acceptance of the Redeemer as having died to save us from our sins, as if mere faith were adequate to save. Thus while it apparently called upon man to choose the difficult way, the way of the cross, the old theology really exacted little of man; it was content with the milder or negative virtues.

The newer theology expects everything of man, just because it is positive. We now see clearly that only so far as we come out of the strongholds of our self-righteousness and really live by the faith we profess, do we make any true headway. For no one died to save us from making this effort. There is no salvation through death alone. It is not a question of the sufferings upon the cross, or even of the resurrection; but of what followed through the triumphant life of the living Lord, whose second coming is through the inner Word. The union of the divine with the human was positive. It was a dynamic, live-giving unity. It meant a new centre of action in the spiritual life of the race. We have been waiting all through the centuries for the time when Christianity should be put to its true test as a dynamic faith.

So, too, the new birth is a positive event in the life of the soul. It begins in all seriousness when we come out into the clear light of day, out of hypocrisy, and every device through which we pretend to be what we are not. Through the new birth, man is made constant. The will and the understanding are brought into efficient unity. Love comes to its own as the greatest power. To love in fulness or consistency means to set ourselves in motion to achieve what we love, namely, to attain truth, to work for it; to serve our fellow men, to show by our conduct that we really love the Lord. In short, the new birth comes, not to destroy, but to fulfil; and to fulfil is to attain the affirmative.

Since so much depends on this advance from the subjective into the objective, every constructive thought, emotion or act of will, is a help. Strictly speaking, every thought is negative or affirmative. By shifting the emphasis or even by changing a word in a sentence, we can change from the negative to the affirmative. With a mere word or intonation, as we address ourselves to a person in spiritual need, we may turn the tide. The idle words for which we are called to account are the negative words, the quick, harsh judgments, the adverse criticism, the hate, anger, jealousy, bitterness, complaint, faultfinding.

Every one whom we thus condemn needs our encouragement and love. A mere hint, a word of good cheer or wise counsel, will sometimes give the impetus. Idle indeed are many of our utterances in comparison with what our language might be.

A mother's loyalty to her children under condemnation is a typical instance of the affirmative attitude. When the heart is affirmative, its power is carried to another, though no word be spoken. We feel the adverse influence of one who does not understand and is condemnatory, one who stands off and inspects. But sympathy is affirmative. We are quickened into productivity by those who believe in us, who call us out and encourage us to do our best without bestowing credit which does not belong to us.

To take the affirmative attitude toward people, is to see the good in them, what they are endeavoring to achieve. This is no small attainment, in view of all that we know about human frailties and sins. We have been apt to think that we should dwell on the frailties and sins, condemn people for them, and call our neighbors to account. But we have excelled in negative criticism. We have left people disheartened. Doubtless they were already keenly aware of their failings. Without being blind to their faults, what is incumbent upon us is to see through these to the goal or purpose in life. To dwell on the process instead of the end, is to be negative. After all, what is worthy of us as lovers of our fellow men, is to see the spirit through the flesh and call the spirit into power.

If no man sins with his whole nature, if there is always a secret place where the Lord dwells, where the Lord may be found, then to be affirmative is to see man in the image and likeness of God; to stand for this ideal, to believe in it, help to call it into realization. That surely is what we wish people to do for us. When disheartened, there is help for us if we once more discriminate between the process and the product, if we return to the ideal, rise above the actual, throw off the bondage of circumstance. Accordingly, we recall what we started out to accomplish. We seek the positive lessons of our present experience. Thus we gradually shift the emphasis, gain a new impetus and begin again. What we thus accomplish for ourselves, we may help others to accomplish by regarding them in the light of their aspirations.

In deepest truth, the divine life within us is seeking to lift us into fulness of being. We have made great headway if able in some measure to distinguish between the human and the divine. Thus to discriminate, in the newer sense of the word, does not mean to put God far from us, because unlike us in nature. Although differing from us in power, God is made one with us by His love. The truth of the incarnation, of the Divine in the human, is affirmative. The great truth is that the presence of God is life-giving, dynamic. It is the presence of God, when recognized in this, its vitalizing aspect, which develops the affirmative attitude in us.

People have thoughtlessly fallen into the habit of speaking of evil as if it were a cosmic power, as if it were co-extensive with the good and at war with it, endangering righteousness, making heaven a matter of doubt. In contrast, goodness appears to be negative; people who are trying to live righteously are often spoken of with disparagement, as if they had chosen the doubtful side. Now, life is oftentimes a warfare within the soul. But we cannot for a moment entertain the hypothesis of failure. The structure of the spiritual cosmos is moral. Life is for moral ends. The destructive forces of the world are in the last analysis negative, despite all appearances. Over against them is the supreme fact of the incarnation with its victory over selfishness. We renew our ideals, and, by an act of faith, cross from the negative to the positive side and ally ourselves with the powers making for righteousness. We refuse to judge by appearances. Belief in the moral integrity of the cosmos is, we see, essential to victory. We are assured that the right will triumph. We identify ourselves in spirit with it. To make this venture is to find ourselves greatly heartened.

The application of the foregoing to daily life becomes the more plain as we realize our responsibility. Simply to think the matter out, is to make headway. By every constructive thought, we help. By every aspiration in love to the Lord, we put ourselves in line with forces able to resist the negative element in us, to overcome the destructive forces. We realize how true is the statement that man is held in equilibrium between the two groups of forces until he makes the choice. Moral choice is an affirmative. By making it, we put ourselves in line with any number of fortunate consequences. This is where we have the greatest power, in this ability to shift the emphasis, to turn from doubt to willingness to believe, from hate to love, and so on through an almost endless series of contrasts.

The dependence of the human upon the divine is seen at every stage. "Lord, I believe; help thou mine unbelief." I do not wholly see. Oftentimes I am very uncertain. I do not know how my wants are to be provided for tomorrow or next year. But there is work on hand for today. Let me act in full faith now. What now seems impossible will prove perfectly possible when the right time comes. I need not hesitate to cultivate and use my powers to the full. Every power is good in its place. The whole of our earthly life is a venture in behalf of faith, to find out what actions are in line with the divine providence and hence are constructive, what ones spring from our self-love and so are destructive. The divine is with us to build us into houses not divided against themselves, to quicken us to serve one Master, one Lord; to guide us into the affirmative, out of all these weaknesses which cause our misery and our discontent. Although we see this great truth only in part and still in a glass darkly, we may declare that we believe. "Lord, I believe; help thou mine unbelief."

X

THE QUICKENING WORD

It is the spirit that quickeneth; . . . the words that I speak unto you, they are spirit, and they are lift.—John vi, 63.

What marvellous words are these that fall from the Master's lips after he has assured his hearers that he is "the bread of life," "the living bread" from heaven, bringing life from the Father and giving life to those who are responsive. Even the words he utters are spirit and life. Hence Jesus says to the disciples on another occasion, after conversing with them at length, "Now ye are clean through the word which I have spoken unto you" (John xv, 3). The word of the Lord then is purifying as well as life-giving. This is the word which "shall not pass away," the word of eternal life, the truth which sets men free. It is the word which unites, which is from the Father to the Son, and thence to the disciples. "If a man love me, he will keep my words: and my Father will love him, and we will make our abode with him . . . and the word which ye hear is not mine, but the Father's which sent me" (John xiv, 23-

24). "For I have given unto them the words which thou gavest me; and they have received them, and have known surely that I came out from thee, and they have believed that thou didst send me" (John xvii, 8).

Is it possible for us to read these same words so that they shall become to us words of spirit and of life? Surely, if we give thought to the inward man as renewed and quickened by the Divine Presence through the creative word.

The Apostle Paul speaks of having "the mind of Christ," which renews. Writing to the Corinthians he says, "But though our outward man perish, yet the inward man is renewed day by day" (II Cor. iv, 16). He also bids the Ephesians seek the inward source of the life that renews. "And be renewed in the spirit of your mind" (Eph. iv, 23). One's prayer would naturally be that of the psalmist, "Create in me a clean heart, O God; and renew a right spirit within me" (Ps. li, 10). This quest for the renewing word reminds us of the inspiriting statement in Isaiah, "But they that wait upon the Lord shall renew their strength; they shall mount up with wings as eagles; they shall run, and not be weary; and they shall walk, and not faint" (Isaiah xl, 31).

Surely, these are wonderful words of promise. God is the true source of strength, of quickening power. Our part is to seek the sanctuary of the

Spirit, that we may truly "wait on the Lord," may hear the quickening word which especially meets our need. Every true prayer should bring this quickening. Whenever we read the Master's words as *words of life,* we ought to be renewed. This renewal ought not only to give us a new impetus to do our work in the world but a sense of power in carrying out that impetus, in His name.

Why is it that we do not more frequently feel this renewing sense of Life? Is it because we read with doctrinal interests and forget to realize that there is quickening value in the very words themselves, in addition to the truth which appeals to our understanding? Is it because we have heard and read these words so many times that now they are as familiar as the beauties of spring or the glories of sunset? Do we read them as historical statements simply, and fail to make them vivid and real in the concrete imagery of our own thought? Or is our failure due to the fact that we have never thought of these words of power as applying to the whole of life, as bringing strength and overcoming weariness through the spirit they bring?

Whatever the reason for failing to make the spiritual word a vitalizing power, it is well to consider the matter in some detail, that we may make headway at last in passing beyond the mere letter.

How can it be true that the inward man is renewed day by day? Through the continuous, the constant presence of the Divine life within us as an influx or incoming into "the secret place" of the heart. While we are not conscious of this incoming Life in the moment of its imbuing touch with our spirit, we may complete in thought what is lacking in actual experience, thinking of it as more immediately present to our spirits at certain times than at others. We may remind ourselves, for example, that during sleep we may be more receptive than in our waking hours, when mental life surges forward so actively. If tonight I take my problems and trials to bed with anxious and fear-breeding thoughts, I shall thereby put a barrier around the inward man. But if I begin half an hour before the time for sleep approaches to make my spirit ready for sleep, I may be able to drop all cares with a free-mindedness which will make of my night's rest a divine communion. My part is to cut connection with external matters, to drop all difficulties and uncertainties, and give myself to gentle sleep, "Nature's sweet restorer," as I would offer my spirit in the truest prayer.

I do not assume to know my chiefest needs in so doing. I do not necessarily ask for help. My hope is that I shall give myself to renewing slumbers in whatever way I need most to be receptive. I return to the sources. I am a child again. If I knew precisely by what word to utter or express this responsiveness at its best, I would let this be my last active thought before giving myself to sleep. I can but say, "Let the words of my mouth, and the meditation of my heart, be acceptable in thy sight, O Lord, my strength, and my redeemer." "The words of my mouth" here represent the external life, while the meditation of the heart stands for the inner self. May these be in unison. May I so give myself in spirit to my Father who knows all my needs that on awakening there will come a new impetus for the dawning day.

Sometimes the day begins to dawn on our consciousness before we open our eyes to behold the beautiful morning light. We may awaken at an earlier hour than usual, to find the mind partially illumined by thoughts which come spontaneously; not by self-conscious exertion, inference or reasoning, but through the divine light. Difficulties are sometimes cleared away in a flash during such an experience. We may see precisely where we have lost the spirit and become immersed in forms, things and processes. We may have a new vision of the self or of some one whom it is our privilege to help.

No rule for putting the mind into this illumined state at its best can be given. One can only say, Cherish it when it comes, observing the conditions which invite its coming that you may encourage their recurrence. By such an experience one learns in part what it means to "think with the spirit" rather than with the external mind. Thus one has a clearer idea what the spirit is.

But one can give a rule for mental states in which the will plays a part. When you are nonplussed, absorbed in conditions, involved in routine and weary, seek some form of recreation or change which will fill your mind for the time, so that you will drop your cares and problems. Then in the midst of it all you may gain the needed contrast, side lights may fall upon your daily life, your work, your relation to your associates. Again, read a favorite author or the Bible until a thought appeals to you with clarifying power and gives you a clue. The Apostle Paul says, "Be ye transformed by the renewing of your mind, that ye may prove what is the good, and acceptable, and perfect, will of God" (Rom. xii, 2).

It is well to bear in mind, also, that there is with us a "spirit of truth" which will lead us into all truth if we faithfully follow. Oftentimes we are unable to find a clarifying or uplifting thought until we first think matters over, looking back over the past to see what influences have brought us where we are today, what lessons are to be learned, what change we need to make in our attitude. There is great value in facing life as it actually exists in the living present which is for our development, noting motives, desires, the kind of love which is prevalent. For when we trace our activities to their sources, seeing clearly, realizing where we weakened, when we became unduly absorbed in externals—then we realize that there is a great freeing power in spiritual truth. Sometimes a thought suffices to turn the prevailing attitude from negative to positive. Sometimes, too, we are prompted to utter the word of power which as quickly sets another free.

It is interesting and helpful to put ourselves back in imagination into the time of the Gospel works of healing and realize what faith was sometimes felt in the Master's presence. One woman of strong faith simply begged leave to touch the hem of Jesus' garment, that she might be made whole. Another person said confidently, "Speak the word, only, and my servant shall be healed." Many of the hearers of the parables and the Sermon on the Mount must have realized most vividly that they were hearing words which were spirit and life. Undoubtedly these hearers felt marked spiritual benefit from these power-carrying words.

Why is it that the followers of Christ in the churches have lost the ability to put the soul in touch with spirit and life as the glad messages once brought power to men? Why was it necessary for a new movement to spring up outside of the churches to re-emphasize the therapeutic value of the Gospel? Apparently because so much stress has been placed upon the intellectual value in contrast with the life-giving power. It has seemed to believers in doctrines that they have done their part when they have come forth into public acceptance of the denominational faith. But thus to believe, with qualification after qualification, lest one fail to state this faith in precisely the right way, has been to lose the force of the original truth. That truth was spread abroad in its universality. It was for every emergency and every hour of need. It was to be made concrete, carried out into the flesh, the external life. When we qualify, when we try to manage or regulate, we check the incoming life, losing impetus and becoming absorbed in our own states and thoughts. But this life comes to us that we may not only receive in fulness but give in abundance.

"Give, and it shall be given unto you." The power of love is increased within us by giving. Conjunction with God is increased through such responsiveness and expression. This reciprocal action is the real test of belief. Man is so constituted as to receive the divine life in ever-increasing fulness and perfection, if he gives in equal abundance. "Every faculty can enlarge . . . with capacity for the receptivity of love and wisdom, peace and joy, which will increase with every influx of life from the Lord." Man appropriates life and power from this influx by living in large-minded responsiveness in accordance with it. The influx vivifies in accordance with reception. Inasmuch as no two individuals are precisely alike, each one needs to learn from experience how to adapt life in its fulness to receptivity and giving. The individual who has proved the power of the quickening word by admitting it into his whole being, is able to speak and to give persuasively to others.

The denominational Christian is apt to become crystallized in attitude through constant emphasis on his particular creed. Hence it remains for the outsider to practice the Gospel with respect to its larger application. But the large-minded follower of Christ never allows his thought to become crystallized at all. There ought to be new evidences, fresh reasons, immediate contacts with life, to keep the spirit alive. This would be our constant effort, if instead of believing for our own salvation or worshipping to increase personal piety, and the mere giving of intellectual assent to what we already believe, we should seek the words of life and of the spirit, and forthwith carry them to someone in need.

Sometimes, in endeavoring to be helpful to one in need, we find it necessary to utter keen truths that arouse dissent, stir the mind into self-defense, or even evoke vigorous emotions in protest. For there must first be vital response of some sort. Thus a physician may find it necessary to arouse a bedridden invalid out of easy-going habits of months or years of self-absorption and the nourishing of luxurious aches and pains. Thus the whole world had to be aroused from its complacent, luxurious and pleasure-loving slumbers by the great war. And the war itself was hardly enough. It had to be followed by other deep stirrings over social issues, strikes and revolutionary programs. "Where there is life there is hope." There must often be ploughing and harrowing. Then we may sow the good seed. All these processes are mentioned in the Gospels, that we may understand the rightful place of the quickening word.

Of what avail after all is belief in spiritual things unless we realize that the spiritual element in us is the life-element, that to be spiritual is to be unselfish? If the divine life which comes to us comes as *power to do,* as energy wherewith to achieve, then the first question is, What is there within our being, our thought, our affections and conduct, which interferes with this life, and how can it be removed?

When such searching questions are put to us we are apt to rise up in self-defense at first. Some of us chanced to have a weak physical inheritance, with tendencies to disease, and so we seem to be exempt. Others are handicapped through early training at home, by educational deficiencies, and by our contact with the world. The story of our handicaps seems indeed endless, as one after another we come forward to tell why we are wearied, burdened, ill and suffering. We seem to be involved in one another's burdens to the limit. Our good resolutions and efforts should have been made by our great-grandparents on both sides of the house. There seems to be no real relation or correspondence between what we inwardly will to be and the conditions which our outward life attracts.

Yet what shall we do? Shall we simply excuse ourselves and our immediate ancestors, making no effort to live by the quickening word? Of what meaning is this great truth that the divine love and wisdom are present with us according to our need?

What if we think as little as possible of heredity and external environment, of any and all handicaps, and begin where we are today to give the inner life more and more fully to the divine presence? However old we may be according to the calendar, whatever the hindrances before us, we are all in the same process at one point or another, and we may all begin to emphasize the divine efficiency instead of dwelling on the human process.

Sincerely to believe in the divine influx as a present reality, is to open our spirits in readiness to receive guidance, the word of life and power which is our greatest need today. We should not try to bring the whole of life into line at once. It is well to concentrate upon an immediate opportunity, lifting our spirit into spiritual light that we may be guided. Then our responsiveness will grow from more to more, and we may find ourselves doing what seemed impossible while we dwelt upon our limitations and handicaps.

Something we have gained if we are willing to entertain even the idea that the divine influx is to be regarded as vitally true now, that the living Lord is here with words which are spirit and are life. For theoretical objections will then fall away and we will begin to see that it is a question of our attitude.

On the inward side of our nature at least the correspondence between attitude and what it invites is perfect. There is all the power and life, all the wisdom and love we need. There is spiritual health and freedom. There is power to live the good life. Everything depends on the human side on recognition of and co-operation with the one Efficiency. We can hardly expect what we have not invited. We are not likely to seek to be "every whit whole" even in spirit, until we gain the idea that the living Christ comes to minister to the whole individual.

So, too, when we read the Gospels, much depends on what we look for. If we, when we read, when we worship, merely anticipate a Sabbath rest from our week day problems, this pleasant contrast is what we are likely to find. If we search the Bible in quest of passages to confirm a favorite doctrine, we may find what we seek. But to find the hidden truth in the letter of the Word, we must make the effort which leads to it. And so to hear the word which is spirit and is life we need especially to start with the thought of God as the living, present Lord, the light of Christ in the soul of man today. We need the idea of the divine influx and with this the thought that there is wisdom, life, power according to our need. The word is a symbol or sign of this power. The idea is a clue or incentive to start our spirit into activity in the direction in which we need light. And so we endeavor to penetrate behind the intellectual form in an attitude of openness of spirit. It was in this penetrating, vivifying spirit that Jesus spoke to the disciples and then said to them in confirmation, "Now ye are clean through the word which I have spoken unto you."

And it is in further confirmation and quickening power that he also says, "And the word which ye hear is not mine, but the Father's which sent me."

XI

WITH SIGNS FOLLOWING

"And they went forth, and preached everywhere, the Lord working with them, and confirming the word with signs following."—Mark xvi, 20.

Oftentimes when reading the Bible we come upon a verse or phrase which we have passed by a hundred times without even noting that it was there, so intent are we ordinarily in the pursuit of those ideas which habit has taught us to look for. There is such a phrase in the verse quoted above, "the Lord working with them," as the clue to the conclusion which follows, "and confirming the word with signs following." We are apt to overlook this significant statement because conventional thought emphasizes belief and the unfortunate consequences of wrong belief. Just above there is a verse which reads, "He that believeth and is baptized shall be saved; but he that believeth not shall be damned." The reader who is fearful of results likely to attend refusal to believe will probably stop at this word "damned," not knowing that this is too strong a word to translate the original, which means "condemned," and is the same word used elsewhere to indicate the natural consequences of our actions. Missing the point with regard to belief, the reader is likely to go on to this last verse, "And they went forth and preached everywhere." This verb "preach" is apt to suggest something modern, and so the whole thought of these verses may be shifted to the dogmas one is supposed to believe or be punished, the dogmas which are commonly preached in the churches.

But, noting this profound statement, "the Lord working with them," we are sent back to reconsider. This is the last utterance of the disciple who writes this Gospel. The evangelist has been telling about the resurrection as the last of those memorable experiences which brought near to men's hearts the power of the Christ over outward things. He informs us very briefly concerning the final appearance of the Master among the eleven. Once more he tells us how the disciples were imbued with the spirit of Christ and sent forth to labor in the vineyard of the Lord. The disciples were not bidden to "preach" in the sense in which we usually apply the term, but "to proclaim the glad tidings to every creature"—this is the way the original reads. It was above all a question, not of alleged punishment to be inflicted on those declining to believe; for this would be a negative consideration; but of the signs following upon belief. What kind of signs were these to be? Not theoretical matters, not the issues which pertain to dogmas and the organization of churches; but practical results. In the name of Christ the disciples were to cast out devils, speak with new tongues, take up serpents, drink deadly things without injury. That is, the disciples were to enjoy those experiences which show the supremacy of the Spirit over material things. More important still, those who believed were to lay hands on the sick, and the sick were to recover. This much having been given as a promise, the evangelist goes on to tell us that the Lord "was received up in heaven." This did not mean that the Master of life and death departed from the disciples, for there follows this phrase so easily overlooked, "the Lord working with them."

Here was an advance even beyond the power of the Master's reappearance among the disciples. The Lord was still present with those who believed and went forth to proclaim the glad tidings with faith that practical benefits would follow among the suffering, and it was because He worked with them that the word was confirmed and the signs were added. This "word" which was confirmed was the glad tidings of the living Gospel. It was confirmed because the Lord worked with the faithful, and produced the "signs following."

This teaching puts belief in an entirely different light. It is plainly not a question of what men proclaim with their lips. Nor does it turn upon what men accomplish in their own might. People have fundamentally misunderstood the Gospel who have been guided by the instruction of the churches concerning doctrines. The living Gospel which the Master taught and exemplified by works was essentially a gospel of works or signs following. It was so understood by the disciples. It was proclaimed and verified by the impressive works of which we read in the book of Acts. It was taught in this way by the Apostle Paul, despite the fact that he was also the first Christian theologian and was inclined to be doctrinal. And then little by little the original Gospel of immediate deeds among the suffering was lost in the maze of doctrinal entanglements.

Looking back to this last meeting of the eleven with the Master and trying to regain the lost clue, we realize that if the gospel of works shall have vital meaning for us there must be a way in which the Lord works with every genuine believer today so as to confirm the word with signs following. This promise is given in connection with all the evangelist has told us about the supremacy of the Spirit over material things. Death apparently made no difference then, and makes no difference today. Time makes no difference. The ages that have come and gone have not separated us from the living Christ. The Lord working with us is still the power that accomplishes the signs that follow. We make a mistake if we allow anything whatsoever to stand between us and the living Lord.

Why is it that we should look for such signs following as the Gospels tell us about? Why has the theologizing world separated sin and sickness, and limited the work of the churches to the kind of preaching that is supposed to show salvation from sins merely? Why have we failed to understand the works recorded in the Gospels in which the healing of disease and the forgiving of sins are brought into intimate relation?

Because, for one thing, we have failed to trace out either sin or sickness to its interior sources. The word translated "sin" in the Gospels means error or mistake, and comes from a verb signifying to miss the mark, that is, fail of doing, fail of one's purpose. To hit the mark would be to realize one's purpose, do one's work in the world constructively. Hence the Master summoned men and women to be whole, to be their true full selves. What does it mean to be sick? In the passage in which Jesus said, "They that are whole need not a physician; but they that are sick," the word rendered "sick" is from a term meaning "to cause evil," of a bad quality or disposition. Evidently the reference is to the mode of life which underlies sickness, the inner state with which the outer is in correspondence. Immediately after saying that it was the sick who had need of him, Jesus said, "I came not to call the righteous, but sinners to repentance." Righteousness is justice, integrity, wholeness of life; it is hitting the mark. Sickness is due to any quality in the disposition which keeps one from attaining this wholeness. The power of the Lord working with us to confirm the word with signs following is the power which seeks to make men whole, whether their lack of integrity is called sin or sickness. Wholeness is a positive consideration.

What kind of sign should we look for, therefore, among those who believe as the Gospels would have men believe? Plainly, that kind of life out of which righteousness or health would spring as a consequence, instead of sin and sickness. The human spirit is made for integrity or wholeness. It has power to hit the mark, to realize life's purpose. Our thought should be given to the conditions which favor such wholeness, we should look for power in this direction. The Lord is working with us in this endeavor.

We have been taking our clues from the sorrow and misery, the sin and suffering of the world.

We have judged the human spirit by its failures, by unfortunate inheritances, by external environment with its sinful influences. But this is wrong. We should think and will and work in the vineyard of the Lord with the divine standard of health or wholeness in mind. It is those who lack the ideal of this wholeness to whom the Gospel comes especially, calling them to turn about (repent) and look towards the light. The Gospel is not a mere corrective of our errors, not a mere plan of salvation. It discloses the true positive plan of living. This plan implies the supremacy of the Spirit over material things. That is, it leads us to the great truth that all real causality is spiritual, that we live and work from the spiritual world, the Lord working with us.

What does the power of the living Christ within us endeavor to achieve? To touch anything in our disposition, such as a tendency to rebel, look on the dark side, work for our own selfish interest, or work against our rivals, so that this lesser activity shall be enlarged into the greater and become constructive. To shake us out of our apathy and self-righteousness, our mere contentment when things are moving as we would like them whether other people suffer or not. To call us into the active service of spreading the glad news for those who believe. To quicken us out of our hypocrisy and every other form of two-fold-ness into true unity within the self, unity between head and heart, the understanding and the will. To prompt our hearts to change from self-love and love for the world to love of God and our fellowmen. To lead us into the true life of charity which is the real sign that we profoundly believe and expect the signs following.

But why do these states which we are summoned out of underlie both sin and sickness? Because he who is in them is untrue to the divine standard of unity or wholeness. He who is a hypocrite, for example, who is working underhandedly for his own interest while seeming to be virtuous, who strives to serve two masters, is in interior conflict, and such conflict is sickness or sin. It shows itself outwardly in a thousand different ways with as many individuals. The individual is beset within and around by those forces which his inner conflict invites. The outward life manifests by correspondence the inner struggle. It is marked in the face, or in the voice. It is expressed in daily conduct, with its subtleties and compromises. It affects the nervous system, and consequently the bodily activity in general. The house thus divided against itself tends to fall. It is repaired and propped up, painted other colors and in various ways disguised. But still it remains the same house. Some onlookers advise changes here. Others suggest modifications there. The external signs or defects appear to be the real trouble. But the real trouble is hidden far within and for that there is no lasting remedy save through becoming a house at harmony with itself—unified, stable, constant.

We are apt to think that the inner pain or struggle is due to some hostile force striving with us, as a germ might play havoc with disordered tissues or a devil insinuate sly temptations. It is great glad news indeed that there is no other life or power in the world plotting and working against man, whatever the appearance and secondary struggles, but only the force of his own self-love reinforced by the self-love of others ignorantly and foolishly laboring against man's own better self, producing out of this inner conflict the whole trouble of the house divided against itself. For with this discovery comes the knowledge that conflict can be changed into harmony through turning about and working with the power once opposed. The living Lord is with those who believe in the sense in which the Gospels teach belief: to bring about just this marvellous sign following, thus turning a state of war into a state of peace so that the supposed enemy is seen not to exist at all.

It seems almost unbelievable at first, that our real foes are those of our own household and that they may one and all be turned into friends. Our conflicts are so real to us and our struggles often so intense that we appear to be mere victims of outward things, as if we were supremely innocent. We do indeed take on by inheritance and from the influences coming from the world those conditions which outwardly speaking give us our experience. Thus, for example, the world readily contributes to the cantankerous person things enough to be cantankerous about. It is not slow in helping the pessimist to find facts to judge in the darkest light. He who has a chip on his shoulder will find other fighters ready for him. The world seems no better to any one of us than we are ourselves. No one can complain that things are not what they appear to be, for the human mind is so constituted as to let the inner state color the world according to its kind. The world corresponds in marvellous degree, even to our fluctuating moods. If we persist in putting the blame on people and things, on God and this splendid universe wherein we live, why then the world will gratify us in our delusion. But there is only one thing to consider after all, and that is our own state of development with the fears it brings, its illusions, its errors, hardships and miseries. There can be no relief save through a change within, since this is the very nature of life, the law of experience. There is no mystery, surely nothing to complain about;

simply the glad news that the key to the whole solution is within ourselves, that the living Lord holds this key with outstretched hand saying, "Come unto me, all ye that labor and are heavy laden, and I will give you rest."

What is it that we need rest from? Is it from ourselves? No, from the inner struggle which we make by going counter to our nature. The nature of man is to find his place in the Grand Man, in the social order in which all who love the Lord and their fellow men are "members one of another." The nature of man is to do a specific work in the world, to be contributory, to co-operate, live and let live, give full measure running over in his desire to serve. The right attitude to take toward our fellow men is to see this tendency toward co-operative service and mutual love working its way out into expression. The living Lord is with every one whom we would help to accomplish just this purpose. That is the great consideration when disciples are sent forth to proclaim the glad news, with signs following.

Are we able, in the first place, to see the significance of the word which shall be confirmed by the signs following? It means a radical change in our thinking for most of us. Our whole habit of thought tends toward emphasis on things, on outward conditions. We say, "human nature cannot be changed," meaning by "human nature" all the sinfulness and criminality, all the selfishness of the world. We say this is impossible. We must take the world as it is. It is full of selfishness and sorrow, and all we can do is to "look out for Number One." Over against this scepticism the Gospel gives its amazing promises: With man such things are impossible, but not with God. "All things are possible to him that believeth." Only believe. Have faith. It shall then be possible even to move mountains. To be saved through belief is to be lifted out of this sceptical attitude into alert expectancy which encourages us to look for the signs following. Such belief is "in His name." It comes with the promise of the spirit of truth present with us to lead us into all truth. It comes with the impetus to go forth into all the world and proclaim with conviction this glad news. Then the Lord will work with us to achieve results which apparently were utterly impossible. Material things will no longer seem to be obstacles in our path. What seemed like a deadly thing will not now prove so. Our hands shall be imbued with power. We will speak with new tongues. All these signs shall come to those who believe whole-heartedly in such a way as to look for benefits coming to others, not the private joys supposedly vouchsafed to the "saved." This is salvation and very much more. It follows the resurrection of man's true self. It is the triumph of the Holy Spirit in us, the work of the ever-living Christ.

XII

THE VALUE OF DENIALS

Many devotees of mental healing believe there is a short cut to the curing of disease through the practice of denials. The word "denial" is not to be understood in the Christian sense of self-denial, losing the self that one may find it, but in the sense of a declaration that any alleged enemy, error or evil does not exist. The first proposition about life in general is, "All is good," and the next, "There is no evil." Radical believers in this method deny even the existence of the body and the natural world. While on the face of it such denials seem absurd, we may well ask ourselves what is the value of this method from a practical point of view.

The theoretical basis of these denials is as follows. Man has two selves or minds, the spirit which is never sick, which never sins or errs; and "mortal mind" or the consciousness of error, the intellect or false mind, always in process of change, essentially external and dependent on information gathered through the physical senses. These senses are discounted as giving misinformation merely, since "there is no intelligence in matter." It is in this false or mortal mind that all error resides. Disease, being an "error of mind," its cure consists in denying not only its alleged power over the flesh but even its existence.

The use of denials is that one may realize "our oneness with God." Otherwise stated, denials are for the sake of affirming the reality of the true self, which is pure spirit, never afraid, never disturbed, never selfish, never at fault. In case of any alleged material force, any cause for fear, any supposed selfishness, one should positively and persistently deny its power, reality or existence. One should deny the existence of all evil, because there is but one Power in the universe and that Power is wholly good, and "all is good." One should deny the reality of all pain, sickness, poverty, old age, suffering, even the reality of death; since these have no existence in Spirit. One ought also to deny the existence of all things which appear to be apart from Spirit, for only Spirit and its manifestations exist. To deny is to efface, blot out the mental pictures, banish the fear, take the life out of adverse suggestions by a counter-suggestion, and overcome all "paralyzing negations." To deny the evil is to affirm the good. To deny pain and sickness is to affirm health. To deny weakness is to realize strength. To deny poverty is to affirm prosperity.

By denying the reality of what seems to exist to mortal sight one realizes what eternally exists, the unchangeable reality of Spirit. It is all a question of realization, not of growth. There is no evolution or progressive change from lower to higher stages. Man does not learn anything from experience, but already *is* in deepest truth what he seems to acquire. All ills are imaginary. There is no reason for learning from experience, since man contains all wisdom within. Man already possesses perfect love and peace. Hence he may unqualifiedly say, "I am spirit, perfect, harmonious, wise, in perfect health, in perfect peace."

Life on this basis would be "the constant recognition throughout the day of the non-reality of the material, knowing that as it is not real, the material man cannot do anything, say anything or think anything; that it is only illusion, appearance having no basis in reality, and that the only thing that takes place is the steady disappearance of this illusionary sense through the action of God." "When you see someone in pain, instead of thinking of him as in pain and so increasing it, turn in thought to heaven and realize that there is no such thing as pain there, and then think of the absolute joy, bliss and happiness in that perfect world."

The first observation to be made is that healers

who have adopted these denials have often met with more immediate success than other therapeutists who raise objections to denials on the ground that they are not true. Outwardly such healers are very prosperous. Their business arrangements are uncommonly good. They are highly contented with the commodities and incomes of the material world. Not concerned with the inconsistencies of their several propositions in contrast with their delight in this world's goods, they concentrate upon those suggestions which bring the most fruitful results. Psychologically speaking there is a great advantage in concentration. To hold absolutely to your point is to succeed where people fail who lose headway when interested in noting what is inconsistent.

We are all placed at times where denials are in order. When face to face with an enemy likely to conquer us if we are not uncommonly skilful and alert, we must resolutely declare that he cannot, must not win. Thus a denial is a psychological device adopted for the time being to get us out of a tight place. A hard-pressed nation may even deny the victories which an enemy is winning, for the sake of keeping up the courage of the people at home. But the question is, What of the day of reckoning? Is it possible to use a denial for the moment, then return to facts and truths? May one adopt denials for the sake of concentration without giving the mind over to extravagances tending toward Oriental pantheism and the relegation of the natural universe to the category of illusion?

It was P. P. Quimby who introduced the distinction between the "scientific man" with the wisdom of Christ to draw upon and the "man of opinions," always changing, subject to errors, fears, and other false beliefs. Dr. Quimby's silent realization consisted in making a clear-cut separation between the two minds. All later disciples of the silent method have made an equivalent separation in their own terms. The mind that is swayed by opinions is the "carnal mind," and to be "carnally minded is death." It is this carnal-mindedness which Dr. Quimby sought to banish by affirming the reality of the truth which makes men free, the truth we possess when we have the mind of Christ. No one can make much headway in this field without drawing this distinction.

Yet one ought to be intelligent enough to distinguish between opinions and the understanding or intellect. The understanding can be lifted into spiritual light and learn to think truly concerning the information the senses give us and the marvellous universe which God has made. There is no intelligible reason for ignoring the long series of progressive changes from simple to complex, from atom to star, from amœba to man, filled as this ascent is by the wisdom of God. Our part is to learn the order and beauty, the system and power of this great world of nature as it exists in the divine purpose. Then it is our privilege to learn to live by the divine order in a useful manner, in constancy of health, with steadiness of purpose and productive courage.

Whatever the reason for making denials as psychological aids to concentration, in the long run we are all compelled to meet life as it is on this natural plane. The truth which makes us permanently free is the truth which discloses natural existence as it was meant to be for enlightened man, the existence which makes for freedom and development, for health and happiness here on earth. The real error of our carnal mindedness is that the body is unfriendly, is a source of evil and misery, prone to disease, weakening old age and a lingering death. The truth is that man might live in perfect harmony with natural law, might use the body as an entirely harmonious instrument, might conquer every obstacle in the path. This is essentially a spiritual truth. One needs to lift the mind into spiritual light, to perceive it. For it is the spirit alone which is able to use the body aright. There is no reason to deny anything that God has made. The error to be denied, and that most resolutely, is the old notion that God wants us to be sick, that He inflicts suffering upon us for our discipline. There are, then, denials which are true, and we all need to make them and most affirmatively. Yet all the while the ideal is to rise to the level of affirmations with such strength that we do not need to deny their opposites. "Perfect love casteth out fear." If you can realize the protecting power of that love, you need not deny the power of the fear. Later, when you are free and strong, you may return and learn the lesson of your fear.

The same is true in the sphere of moral ideals. The more severely pressed the soldier "who fights the good fight" the less reason he has for admitting the power of evil. There can be no such word as fail in the moral world. We declare that all lying, stealing, dishonesty and wrong-doing shall be overcome, and that righteousness shall prevail. Yet after all what is it that calls out a man's potentialities and makes him a hero in our eyes? Surely not a mere error. It is because he rises to meet a well-nigh insuperable difficulty. We grow strong by meeting opportunities which call us into activity to the full. Sometimes the more valiantly we admit the foe to be conquered the more resolutely we rise to the occasion which "makes the man."

What the moral soldier affirms is that right is

on his side, a right strong enough to conquer any wrong whatsoever. He fights with his spirit. He first conquers the enemy in himself by facing his fears and the possibility of defeat. Then, made alert and affirmative, he goes forth to meet a danger which no denial can minimize but which must be faced to the end. At every juncture when tempted to weaken, he re-affirms the supremacy of the right and bravely presses forward. He cannot for a moment afford to entertain a weakening idea.

Here we have concentration in high degree. Allowing for different conditions, we may think of this valiant moral attitude as applied in the inner world where it is a question of attaining health or healing others. One ought to be as valiant in holding to the Christ ideal as the moral soldier in fighting on the field of battle. For the healer it is a question of the victorious faith which pushes through to the end and overcomes every obstacle.

It is a help in this connection to distinguish between lower and higher levels of mentality. On the lower level with the "mind of opinions" one sees "in a glass darkly." One is then subject to mere reports, haunting fears, besetting illusions, misinterpretations. The worst of these is mistaking this body of flesh and blood for oneself. To be thus minded is indeed to be in danger of spiritual death. On the higher level one seeks to think with the mind of Christ, to live in perfect peace and love, realizing that the soul is a "son of Spirit." The knowledge gained on the higher level is insight "face to face," a vision in which we see the same things but see them as they are.

To disconnect from the activities of the lower level and open the spirit on the higher is to find oneself in another realm of thought. The change from the one to the other is sufficient in itself to set higher activities in motion. For it is a dynamic change. It opens the spirit to the divine influx of love and wisdom. It is man who makes the change. It is God who "giveth the increase." Life "on a purely spiritual basis," then, would be in unison with God, wherever one might be led, whatever the work given our hands to do. When "God and one make a majority" we need no longer deny what is to be overcome. For we now function on the level of constructive forces.

It is plain of course that few of us arc open as we might be on the higher level. Most of us are placed where it is better to admit that we are not as responsive as we might be to the incoming divine life, and then ask what needs to be overcome. The whole secret for us to learn is interior openness and responsiveness, recovery of the open vision which will disclose divine truth. In so far as we are open within and the channels of our being are kept open even from the inmost centre to the outermost parts of the body, we are in perfect health, able to function as free spiritual beings.

A denial, then, is a practical device needed when we are not sufficiently affirmative. A man might, for example, deny evil reports concerning himself, defending himself by arguments, until he realizes that no man need contend with unrighteous judgments but may put his whole reliance on what is true. A person may deny the supposed power of an illness that is attacking him, since he is determined to be well. But later he may learn to unite in thought with the power of God making for health. Later still, his ideal may be to live so that he may let all external circumstances take care of themselves in God's own time. The real point is that external things are occasions simply, while real causes are spiritual: The occasion will make or unmake the man according to his way of meeting it. The opportunity will be a blessing or a curse. Every occasion meant for our betterment may serve to call us into productive activity, if we meet it with wisdom concerning our true place and service in the world. All opportunities are blessings in God's eyes. We have the power to unite our hearts to make them blessings. Everything depends on becoming affirmative. Our affirmations will become more intelligent as we proceed. What would they be if we habitually had the mind of Christ, instead of fluctuating between things carnal and things spiritual?

XIII

SPIRITUAL INFLUX

In another chapter we noted certain of Swedenborg's teachings which point very directly to the theory of spiritual healing. Indeed, there are several lines of resemblance between the doctrines of the great Swedish seer and the modern therapeutic movement. The intimate relationship was quickly noted by W. F. Evans, sometime Swedenborgian minister, when he visited Dr. Quimby as a patient in Portland, in 1863.[1] Mr. Evans's books were widely read by early leaders of the new therapeutism, and so there was a commingling of ideas derived from Quimby and from Swedenborg. The theory, for example, that there is precise correspondence or relationship between spiritual states and natural conditions is due to this commingling. Swedenborg teaches that there is an influx of spiritual life into the human soul, and that our spiritual life is conditioned by our response to this inflowing of power from heavenly sources. He also teaches that many diseases have spiritual causes, and that

1 See "A History of the New Thought Movement," Chap. IV.

salvation from our ills would ensue if we would acknowledge the Divine inflow in such a way as to prepare for genuine regeneration. To the believer in spiritual healing it is but one step further to incorporate this theory of the heavenly influx into the practical teaching known as the New Thought. Hence the new therapeutists are surprised when Swedenborgians fail to apply their teaching in this way.

But to his strict followers Swedenborg seems to be primarily a theologian. Everything in his system turns upon his doctrine of the Lord, the relation of this doctrine to the spiritual interpretation of the Bible, and "the life of charity" which ought to ensue as a result of this acceptance of true doctrine. Hence the prevailing interest is in salvation or regeneration, regarded as superior in importance to "healing." It is the New Church which should assimilate the New Thought, not the other way. Moreover, Swedenborg teachcs that the Lord approves of our use of natural means in the treatment of disease, and this is taken to mean the use of medicine and reliance on physicians. This is why the New Churchman of the doctrinal type turns as readily to medical practice as if he were not a believer in the Divine influx.

The apparent points of contact become radical points of difference, when we compare the views of the typical New Thought devotee with those of the typical Swedenborgian. Where, for example, the disciple of the New Thought would harmonize contrasts the Swedenborgian would strengthen them. Practically everything turns upon the interpretation of Swedenborg's teaching concerning the nearness of the spiritual world to the natural, the theory of "discrete degrees," and the doctrine of contiguity.

In his "Divine Love and Wisdom" Swedenborg teaches that while the spiritual world is indeed intimately related with natural things this intimacy is not the relationship of *continuity,* as the doctrine of spiritual influx would seem to suggest, for this would mean unbroken inflow from the spiritual world into the natural; but is the relationship of "contiguity," or the nearness of things fundamentally unlike. There is a discrete difference between spiritual and natural things. Real causes are spiritual, natural events are effects. There is no interfusion or blending. The same is true of God and man, the Lord Jesus and man. Consequently every comparison should be made clear and distinct. It is especially important to guard against mysticism or pantheism, that is, any teaching which lessens distinctions between God and man, or in any way compromises the doctrine of the Lord. This explains why any teaching not founded on the true doctrine of the Lord seems to a Swedenborgian a "falsity." To advocate spiritual healing by identifying oneself with Christ, or by regarding the human self as a "part of God," would be to err in the very beginning. Any theory or method founded on a "false premise" must itself be false.

It may be seriously questioned, however, whether a mode of inference which so easily dismisses a teaching that has brought incalculable good to thousands of people is fair either to the new therapeutism or to Swedenborg. The literal disciple of Swedenborg, making over-much of the theory of discrete degrees, emphasizes the fact that man is merely a "receptacle" of life. Hence he tends to rear doctrinal barriers where Swedenborg would have called attention to *the mode of life* incumbent upon all who know the glorious truth that man receives "life from the Lord."

We must admit of course that God is the only giver of life. It is plain also that to regard man as a receptacle of Divine life is very different from affirming that the higher self *is* Divine, that man is "one with God," that each of us can become "the Christ;" for from a New Churchman's point of view the whole question is how, given our alienation from the Lord, we can attain unison of will with Him, and there is no advantage in merely affirming what we have yet to achieve. The New Thought devotee appears to attribute the efficiency to man. But Swedenborg teaches that to "look above oneself is to be lifted up by the Lord; for no one can look above himself, unless he is lifted up by Him who is above." Yet when we have noted all these considerations, it may well be that despite doctrinal divergences there are impressive points of resemblance and contact.

Swedenborg teaches that man as he was created might have remained wholly open to the heavenly influx, without disease and without sin. The crucial question then is, Why did man lose his pristine privilege? What may he do to regain it? To learn Swedenborg's answer is to find that the dark picture of man's sins and the hells to which they correspond is not so dark as it seems. For man was created in the Divine image and likeness, this is still the ideal put before man for attainment. To deny the ignorance into which we are born and the darkness in which we find ourselves is not to find the wisdom that we need. But granted fundamental awareness of our actual situation, our great concern is with the wonderful opportunity put before us here in this natural world. Here is the ideal place to meet life fairly and squarely, overlooking nothing, never ignoring the conditions in which we are placed. To look at life courageously and "see it whole" is to realize that each of us has a *prevail-*

ing to him. No device will ever succeed in concealing man's actual self—as if he could somehow avoid facing himself, avoid repenting and coming to judgment.

Despite his suggestive statement about the possibility of human openness to Divine life and what such receptivity would mean in relation to health, Swedenborg does not however draw the inference that man might recover this responsiveness and apply it to the healing of disease. Swedenborg does not teach any method by which a man might put his spirit into a certain attitude to appropriate and utilize the life which enters the spirit from within. He assures us that the mind rules the body by influx, that the body is "mere obedience," and so he seems on the point of saying that man should cultivate the poise and inner control which are essential to intelligent use of the bodily instrument; but he does not touch on these matters. He has nothing to say about "the power of thought" as mental healers employ it. He does not emphasize the importance of mental attitudes, nor teach the art of "attracting success." He has little to say about the imagination and almost nothing about the emotions or the effects they produce. Nor does he write about ideals and the need of affirming them. He makes no reference to the subconscious mind as the term is now used, although he approaches modern physiological psychology at various points.

Indeed, his emphasis is never put on any method employed by man for his betterment. Man of his own volition is said to be tending toward the hell of self-love, and the Divine love alone can bring salvation from this natural tendency toward the hells. What is needed is the doctrine which acquaints man with the subtle influences to which he is subject when withdrawn from the hells through the ministry of angels.

The reason for this apparent neglect of the methods so much in vogue among mental healers is that Swedenborg sees no salvation for man save by admitting sins as *sins,* not as "errors" or illusions. Man has no power of his own to overcome temptations, but may be lifted above them by the Lord's help when he is willing. Man needs to realize his own weakness and unregeneracy, needs to see that there is a discrete difference between himself and the Lord who would save him.

One sees why most followers of Swedenborg have been highly doctrinal in type. The relationship with the Lord is interpreted in a beautiful way, so far as life in general is concerned; hence the nobility of spirit everywhere attributed to Swedenborgians. The emphasis put on "the life of charity" or service according to Divine precepts has always led them to make steady effort to live by their doctrines. But if asked why they do not connect this beauty of spirit with healing for the body, they would point out not only the need for regeneration as above indicated but the fact that there is a break in the correspondences to which man is subject. Man by taking on hereditary evils comes into the world handicapped. Moreover, man through external influx is open to tendencies making for disease and evil through his contact with the world. From this compromised state of things, namely, the conflict between the influxes, there is no escape through any method of healing. While, therefore, the Swedenborgian does indeed believe in the Divine influx with respect to conduct, that is, in the inner life, he finds himself surrounded by a natural environment and a natural inheritance which may be radically unlike his inner state and needs. Where the disciple of the New Thought sees favorable relationships or correspondences only, and affirms that heredity can be overcome and circumstance conquered, the New Churchman points out that there is not necessarily a condition of harmony between inner state and outward condition. Consequently he does not anticipate healing or escape from material conditions.

A few of Swedenborg's readers, however, interested to find those principles which so quickly led Mr. Evans to espouse Quimby's theory and method of spiritual healing, have indicated what to them is a more practical way of accepting the idea of the Divine influx. It is pointed out that as all causes are spiritual, as natural things have no life or power, the relationship of the spiritual to the natural is "dynamic." The Divine influx then is the real causal efficiency in the world, whatever the degree of difference between the spiritual world and the natural. It accomplishes its results despite the contrasts. It attains its ends with man too. It is a real, a vital inflow. Hence we should not emphasize the mere nearness of the spiritual world, pointing to the differences and contrasts; but call attention to the great truth that man lives, moves, and has his being in and from this influent Divine life.

Why then should we always dwell on the fact that man is a "receptacle" of life? The result might be mere acquiescence on our part. What if we emphasize the dynamic character of the Divine influx, seek to unite with it and become affirmative, in co-operative response to the Divine love and wisdom? Indeed, Swedenborg teaches that although man has no life or power of his own he should act "as if" all the power were his —while inwardly acknowledging that it is the Lord's. This would mean that man should actively respond to, assimilate and express the life which comes as love and wisdom. What is needed is a method of realization which will enable man to become a genuinely efficient "organ of life." This efficiency ought to be more practically attained on Swedenborg's basis then on the New Thought basis. For Swedenborg's teaching is more explicit, that is, that the Divine life first touches the will or the affections, and then the understanding or intellect. This means that man more directly receives Divine love than Divine wisdom, that his will is closer than his thought. It is therefore plain that man must first modify his affections before he can rightly reform his thinking. To begin by affirming or holding thoughts would be to put the cart before the horse.

Granted this more interior knowledge of the human spirit, namely, that the life or love is prior to the thought, we are in a position to see the larger meaning of the theory of spiritual healing. For in his development of this theory Dr. Quimby also emphasized the importance of knowing what the life is before one could rightly adjust the thoughts. Not primarily concerned with theological matters, Quimby approached the subject of man's relation to God in a purely practical way. Laying emphasis on the Divine presence as Wisdom adequate to meet all occasions and all needs, he acquired a method of practical realization or silent spiritual healing, and used this method in the healing of disease because this was the work given him to do. He saw that healing included the life, and that it was necessary to change one's idea of God if the idea was ecclesiastical rather than practical; but his province was to make sure that people saw the connection between the Divine presence and healing, since this was the vital application of Christianity which the world had overlooked for eighteen hundred years. The method of realizing the Divine presence which was original with him could be applied with equal value to man's life as a whole.

It was in accord with our practical age that Quimby should bring the psychological elements of this realization into view. Quimby drew a fundamental distinction between the outer man or "man of opinions" and the inner mind which can know the Christ-truth. He believed that by absenting himself from the outward world with its opinions and errors, its notions about disease and suffering, one could unite in spirit with the Divine life ready at hand to guide the way to freedom. To enter vividly into realizations of the Divine presence is to banish every influence to which man is subject through opinion, including hereditary influences and those coming from the world. To "realize" is to become open to the Mind which never changes, whereas the mind of opinions is always changing. Quimby developed these realizations into an effective method of silent or spiritual healing which applied, as he believed, to all kinds of disease and trouble in the world.

The question would then be, How may I put my spirit into the right attitude to receive Divine love and wisdom most effectively? Thus questioning one would find that the way to test any spiritual teaching is by the method of inner experience. In accordance with the modern spirit one would not judge even the scriptural works of healing by any doctrine, but one would be prompted by the endeavor to recover the lost methods of Christian healing. Thus one might make capital use of the idea that the Divine life enters the soul by influx, thence into the understanding, which in turn may be "lifted into spiritual light." One would then turn to the body with the expectation that its ills could be overcome through this inner response to influx.

But what of the distinction between God and man? The answer is that the idea of discrete differences does indeed help us in doctrinal matters, but this idea should not keep us from putting primary emphasis on the love which *unites* and the wisdom which *guides* when man becomes truly receptive. The tendency of the incoming life is to make us in very truth sound men and women in the image and likeness of God. It is this which we should dwell on, this we should recognize, substituting the Divine idea for any other. This tendency is the basis of true spiritual healing because it is the basis of spiritual life. Here is the clue to all real efficiency and *the dynamic attitude.*

The objection to urging discrete differences, and the break in correspondences due to heredity and present relations to the world, is that when we have made all the requisite doctrinal qualifications we are apt to stop there instead of pressing forward to realize what the Divine presence vitally means. If we reduce man to a "receptacle," then leave him there, tied down by qualifying doctrinal distinctions, impotent in thought, almost helpless in will, the prospect is indeed dark. Even the doctrine of the Lord might then remain an intellectual instrument merely. The modern spirit says, If you believe all efficiency is from the Lord, show this by living in accordance with Divine providence as *vitalizing guidance today.* It asks you vividly to realize what it means to attribute all love and wisdom to God, and to apply this realization to all problems. The person who concentrates upon the vital present realization is far more likely to show actual results than one who uses these ideas as doctrines merely.

If charged with exalting the human self unduly, the practical devotee would say, "Whereas I was blind, now I see." I formerly lived in bondage to material things, now I have the ideal of the supremacy of the spirit. Once I believed that sickness, trouble, poverty, weakening old age and an untimely death were the lot of man; now I know that God intended man to be in good health, to increase in power and live a triumphant life. I used to give way to negative attitudes, now I am learning to adopt the affirmative attitude in all things. Anyone can learn how to take this attitude. Everyone can draw on Divine sources at need.

Mental healing devotees do not claim to be theologians. They leave believers in the new therapeutism free to think as they like about God, although steadily insisting that God dwells with man and that we may grow into "the mind of Christ." They sometimes verge strongly toward Oriental mysticism, but this is for the sake of making the Divine presence vivid. They sometimes speak of man as a god, identifying the higher self with Christ, but this is to encourage the individual to recognize his full privileges as a son of God. To condemn the teaching because its statements concerning God are not always satisfactory in form would be to miss the fruits or "signs following" which are the real evidences of the power of this new movement.

There is of course a difference between mental and spiritual healing,. but the latter is meant to include the new birth and the spiritual life. The view of the spiritual life thus emphasized is enriched by the idea of the Divine influx. But as developed by therapeutists this view ordinarily has little to do with psychical experiences and visions. The idea of intuition or direct inner guidance is substituted for that of the Swedenborgian theory of guidance through angels. Nothing is said about three classified heavens and three hells, since the new therapeutists anticipate endless progress in the future life, not a life that is determined once for all by our choice or prevailing love in this world. Consequently the practical worker parts company with the doctrinaire, at all points responsive to the spirit of his age. But his study of the problems of spiritual healing is always fostered by comparison with teachings which have points in common. Hence he is not disposed to be dogmatic or to claim that the account is closed.

If the literal follower of Swedenborg is right, there is little to say in behalf of spiritual healing. But if it be permissible to interpret Swedenborg freely or liberally, then we may profit by the description of life which Swedenborg gives us and wholly assimilate his teaching concerning the Divine influx. Great good might come from interchange of ideas between New Thought people and Swedenborgians. The former need to discriminate more carefully, need light on the more difficult problems of salvation, need to advance from mere healing to the ideal of the completely spiritual life. But the Swedenborgians might well learn to overcome their fears, their bondage to medical practice, their blindness to the practical values of the Divine influx. Both groups of people belong to the new age, and that age is far larger than any doctrinal formulation lets us know. To read Swedenborg literally is to miss the great value of his teaching. But to read him in the modern empirical spirit is to see that the true way to test what he taught is by endeavoring to live in accordance with it, by putting ourselves in dynamic relation with the Divine influx.

XIV

THE INTUITIVE METHOD

WE have now passed in review the method of denials and found a certain practical value in such denials. We have also found practical utility in the idea that love and wisdom are received by the human spirit through "influx." In the one case we have guarded against overdoing mere denials, since the ideal is to rise to a higher level of affirmativeness through union with the perfect love which casts out fear. In the other case we have observed that one should not overdo the idea of discrete differences between God and man, since doctrinal qualifications might mean loss of headway. The ideal is, a dynamic attitude making concentration steadily possible. There is a higher or synthetic attitude which includes the truth of the methods which we have been passing in review. This implies the intuitive method which Quimby's work with the sick disclosed. For many of us this method is still an ideal to grow to through experience. But it is everything to have an ideal.

If mere denial were enough, there would of course be no reason for inquiring into the origin of a man's trouble. If denials sufficed, all we would need would be a complete set of statements covering all cases. We might then proceed on the same theoretical basis with every person. We would never look to experience, for we would not expect to learn anything from it. We would not reason, having first condemned our God-given reason as foreign to spiritual thought.

If, however, we wish to disabuse a patient's mind of its errors and their attendant consequences by leading the sufferer out of darkness into a light that abides, we should seek causes and endeavor to make explanations which really explain. For we should be mindful of the fact that an error merely denied may come back, like a mistake in solving a mathematical problem which we do not understand. We know too that a mind which deceives itself by abstract propositions must sooner or later come down to the concrete. A denial used for practical purposes may be very serviceable. But "a philosophy of denial" is false.

The patient is indeed a sufferer from "error." But the error is that of misinterpretation. There is no more reason for denying the thing interpreted than for denying the existence of an object in the woods mistaken in the dusk for a bear. The courageous thing is to march straight up to the thing, see what it is, see what part of our visual illusion had an objective basis, and what part was attributed to the object by the imagination. Our fear and excitement disappear when we see precisely what is before us, namely, a harmless stump. We have learned something about the tendency of the mind to project its inferences into space. We can no more deny the reality of the external object than that of our own self. The illusion was as real as life itself while it lasted. It would have been a delusion only in case there were no stump or other misinterpreted object.

So in the case of any problem, sin, sickness, or trouble: complete freedom is found through the whole truth. The fact that we possess a higher self that is "never sick" is only one of the essential facts. It is a question of the right interpretation to be put upon the experiences of the self in its long progress into spiritual light.

If, for example, I misjudge a painful sensation due to inward pressure which might be explained by indigestion and attribute my pain to a disordered heart, not to a disordered stomach, I proceed to develop my misinterpretation according to my first error. I then entertain corresponding fears and other exciting emotions, enlarging upon my pain and describing my symptoms to other people. This is what Quimby calls "inventing a disease." But if I had been able to trace the disturbance to its right source, physically speaking, I should at least have avoided the initial error. I might then have proceeded to overcome the disturbance. But my indigestion might have been a mere expression of nervous tension and haste. Behind this there might have been one condition after another. At length I might come to the more interior state which was a prevailing cause of such disabilities. In any case very much depends on the opinion which I associate with my pain. There is a difference between removing the pain for the time being, for instance, by denying its power to cause disease; and endeavoring to live from the higher level so as to avoid all troubles of this sort.

The intuitive method consists in rendering the spirit interiorly open to the inner state in the patient, to discern the actual condition or cause, in contrast with its physical accompaniments. The inner state involves, for example, the person's attitude toward life, his way of taking events, his type of belief, the influence of his disposition or temperament, the use or misuse of his spiritual power. Inasmuch as no two individuals are alike, it is necessary to gain the intuitive impression in each case. Since the patient's condition changes under treatment, there is reason for seeking fresh impressions from time to time. The implied conviction on the healer's part is not merely that he possesses an interior susceptibility to such impressions as experience has tended to make him aware of, but also an interior openness to spiritual guidance. This guidance is an expression of the Divine wisdom for that occasion and that need.

This way of seeking "the mind of Christ" is different from the one which assumes that we already possess that perfect mind in actuality. For one sees that life is too rich in experiences to permit a knowledge of much of it at a time. There is progressive change. There is experience with its opportunities, the lessons it holds for us. There is also an influx of wisdom to meet the need and an influx of power to overcome the obstacle. In short, there is with the human spirit a movement tending to express itself in "fulness of life." We are all at some point in recognition of and response to that life—we who have at least learned not to rebel. The question is, What point? What is the next step? What should be the attitude toward the influent Life even now seeking to lead one in that step? For unless there is change at the centre, in the life or conduct, there will be no real change elsewhere—whatever the denials. With the change at the centre, results are sure to follow. Perfect peace will always cast out fear. Light will always dispel darkness.

Nevertheless, the intuitive method implies the same contrast between the higher level and the lower which is noted by those who give allegiance to denials. Were the healer merely to render his mind receptive to another's atmosphere, he might take on that atmosphere and be unfit for service. While seeking to know how the patient is situated in his darkness, the healer must stand in the light, seeking "the wisdom of the situation." This wisdom should not merely dispel the temporary darkness but show the patient how to take the next step in spiritual development. It is intuition which yields this illuminating clue. The healer believes this insight to be God-sent, impartial, of the nature of that spiritual truth which sets all men free. The objective is to make the sufferer acquainted with spiritual resources, that he too may seek the inner guidance which applies to the occasion.

To be sure, the best way to accomplish the desired result with the patient, so far as the process known as silent treatment is concerned, is to concentrate upon the Divine ideal, to see the patient in spirit as sound, clean, open, free. Here we have affirmation or suggestion at its best. For the eye must be single to the ideal. There must be no compromise. Concentration is essential to dynamic faith.

But the intuitive healer does not stop there.

The conversation which follows the treatment makes plain the causes so as to point the way to permanent freedom. Thus the educational work grows gradually out of the therapeutic work and in the end becomes more important. This involves an explanation of the principles implied in healing. The clue is taken from the actual needs of the patient as intuitively disclosed. The patient is taught to recognize and co-operate with the Divine influent life. He is taught more than mere realization, he is taught how to grow.

If attainment were reduced to mere expression of what is "within," there would of course be no real place for aspiration. It is a question of pressing forward to the open vision. The right attitude having been attained, one ought in truth to grow into abundance and freedom.

Mere affirmation might suffice if we were all alike, as mere "parts of God" as cogs are parts of a machine. But we are all different, and remarkably so. We not only live a life in the world which distinguishes us from all others, but in the inner sanctuary we are still more unlike. The higher we ascend even to the level of the Divine purpose, the more true this is. The very reason for our being is found in the distinctive end to be achieved by and through us. Each of us has a work to do. The guidances that have come to us from the beginning have been given us for that work. Even our mistakes have taught us lessons. The whole meaning of the activity that stirs within us from stage to stage in life's journey, and carries us forward from the present into the future, is just here. It is never a mere question of the guidance as such, as an insight pleasant to have, but of its relation to the needs of the hour in our adaptation to the world. Deny the lower half and you have no subject-matter for experience.

All our experiences are fitting us to do our individual work. We may seem far indeed from that work as we plod along, mistaking our bodies for ourselves, regarding heredity and environment as the leading influences which shape us, meanwhile striving as we do for a living amidst materialistic competition. We may seem equally far from spiritual things when we are ill from diseases which appear to be bodily maladies and nothing more. But anon the intuition of some one gifted in spiritual healing may bring us a new insight. We may come to regard the spirit as the real man. We may see that spiritual influences are real causes. We may learn that heredity and influences coming from the world can be thrown off. Then in time we may come to see the meaning of the long years of our bondage, may see that all our experiences can be turned to account.

The question, Where do we stand? is crucial because the same life which is opposed through ignorance is the Efficiency which will carry us forward to freedom and success. The ideal is to unite with the Divine guidance and move on apace with its rhythms, taking its way for our own, ready to go wherever the leadings shall guide. Each individual must learn this adjustment because no two are alike, no two are placed in precisely the same way. We need the training appropriate to our work.

The advantage of the intuitive mode of statement is that it can be true to all the facts and assign them all to the proper level in such a way as to grant full supremacy to the Divine ideal. Life teaches us that not one step can be omitted. We who are leaders are perfectly aware that this is true. We know that at times we have plodded, at times we have stumbled in the darkness. We learned by doing. We became strong through overcoming, never by ignoring. Sometimes we had to pause, look about and get our bearings anew. Life itself developed a kind of composure and strength in us. Life has quickened us to see the whole situation in which we are placed. Its spontaneous deliverances have greatly surpassed all utterances that we deliberately planned for. Why should we ask for anything less for those whose journeyings have not taken them so far?

What we should in fact strive to attain, when we seek to be of the greatest service, is creative insight into native capacities and talents. The overcoming of diseases is incidental to this. The finding of a way out of sin is secondary. The conquering of poverty and bondage to material circumstance is secondary too. The primary consideration is a person's individuality, the work he can do, the guidance coming directly to him to lead him into that work. To learn this the central state of his life, to see what is in process, what is being disclosed, is to enter sympathetically into his presence as a spirit. Intuitively speaking each of us is being quickened with just the guidance we need, as unaware of it as we may be. The Divine wisdom is latent in the present experience, even in its darkness. This immanent wisdom can be brought to the light. We can be of service in making people aware of this the real life-process. Thus the Divine creative work may be furthered through us.

We all have something approaching this creative insight in what we call heart-to-heart talks with people when it is given us to say the right word. Nonplussed and in eager quest of light, a friend will pour out the heart's sorrows and disappointments. We as listeners may be puzzled at first, at a loss to know what to say. But presently one statement will throw light on another, more light will begin to come, and we will see that our friend had all the elements of the longed-for wisdom but lacked their uniting clue. We are then led to put two and two together, to point to the end all along implied in the rough journeyings, disclose the ideal immanent in the actual. Our insight shows the wisdom for the present need. It calls our friend into power by restoring confidence and yielding vision. Very likely at times in the conversation we speak better than we know. Speaking frankly, we tell plain truths, instead of qualifying them by polite language till all their force is gone. These truths stay with the friend and work for good. Then the guidance comes to him directly, mayhap in the silence of the night when the friend sees the wisdom that is above all human advice.

The intuitive healer goes further than this by directly opening his spirit, by talking from spirit to spirit in that language which the heart knows. He could not thus give his spirit to be a means of guidance to another soul if he intruded any abstract theories of his own. He opens his spirit intuitively afresh, never knowing what may come. He is ready for any guidance, old or new, expected or surprising. His own thought or feeling may be a witness of the Spirit, but he does not claim that he himself is infinite Spirit. He seeks reciprocal union with God, not mere blending with Him. He hopes to be a messenger of "the light of Christ in the soul." He does not pretend to be the Saviour of men. That light is indeed the one which will disperse all darkness, when the right time comes, but it is not a light to be turned on in full force at will as one might illuminate a room by merely pressing a button. The light that shines will be the light needed for the occasion. It will increase and increase without limit.

It once more becomes plain, therefore, that everything depends upon the end we seek, upon what we primarily love. If we still love self and worldly power above the "things of the spirit," then we attribute our efficiency as healers to Thought, we claim everything for the higher self as one with God or a part of Him, we claim the whole end of the spiritual life as achieved now, and we affirm our self-complacent identity with the Christ. We then proceed from one affirmation to another, according to the need. We enter "the silence" to enjoy its gratifying repose and declare our prosperity. In short, we practically make a god of Thought. But if we have genuine love of the Lord in our hearts, then we attribute the efficiency to the Divine presence as love and wisdom, and in our higher selfhood we aspire, we pray, seeking to be led by the "mind of Christ." That is, we desire to grow in intuition through response to Divine wisdom, and it would be absurd to try to grow unless we were actually aware of a deficiency. When at last we realize how little insight we possess and how great is the need to grow in intuition, then indeed there is hope for us.

The intuitive method is the larger, inclusive method which we grow into after a time when we realize the limitations of all methods centring about the human self. The whole idea of intuition involves the thought of the Divine presence as its source, the realization that life is a process or growth and that there is need of guidance all the way along. While the human self seems all-sufficient, it seems possible to ignore life or experience as if it were an illusion. Hence we tend to say with the mere abstract theorist, "Man never learns from experience." But when we return to life and see that man never learned anything whatsoever except through experience, then we begin to acquire that true humility which is the beginning of wisdom, we pray to be rightly led, we accept the dynamic or progressive attitude, casting aside our static abstractions. With this change of heart, a reconstruction of our philosophy follows. Our prayer henceforth is for the wisdom needed for *the next step.* We have no formula to fit the occasion. We have no cut-and-dried method. We do not crystallize our theory into a thought to be affirmed by all alike at a given hour, throughout the month. But we endeavor to lead all who are responsive to seek that Presence whose wisdom is equal to every occasion, well knowing that no two people have precisely the same needs at the same time. "There is guidance for each one of us, and by lowly listening we shall hear the right word."

XV

SPIRITUAL SUCCESS

SUCCESS used to be regarded as a question of conditions and things in the world around. It was frequently said to be a matter of money alone. We were told that "nothing succeeds like success," and that "business is business," as much as to say, the end justifies any means we may see fit to adopt.

Many people may still be inclined to believe that this is the ruling motive, inasmuch as the profiteer is constantly mentioned in the public press. Yet success has become largely psychological, and profiteering itself depends on the popular mind. There is no longer success in general. The man himself is the greatest factor: his starting-point, the obstacles he has to overcome, the methods he has employed, the services rendered, the motives which prompted him. What we long for is success that befits us as men and women, according to our type and the kind of work we choose. We desire success that endures, that makes us free and independent. Such success presupposes the art of life. It is for all who are eager and thoughtful. Success may spring from any conceivable beginning, in any environment.

Success must of course include adaptation to the world in so far as we are led to co-operate with people where they are. We always measure success in part by wage-earning power. We still speak of men who have not "made good," when no financial rewards are forthcoming. But we can no longer single men out as representatives of what we mean by success merely because they have made money. Success is manifold, and we judge by varied standards according to our interest in life. The Salvation Army has faithfully informed the world that "a man may be down, but he's never out." Mere failure is not a test. "It is what man would do that exalts him."

There is a sense in which success cannot be said to have been achieved by society unless all classes share in it. Hence we take little interest in schemes for social revolution in behalf of one class simply. It is surely not a question of "the privileged classes" or favored individuals said to be "lucky" from birth. It is not a question of individuals or classes but of man as a social being, man thinking, willing, doing, living, rounding out his days in the power and beauty of accomplishment.

To say that success cannot be measured by

worldly standards alone is not to plead for a spiritual life by which people console themselves who have failed in the world. Mundane life is of course incomplete, and we anticipate compensations in the future because of efforts which have not yet borne fruits. The spiritual life is always a consolation in a way. But we no longer underrate success in the world as a way of praising people who adopt the spiritual ideal. A failure here would be a failure in the future life, too. It is not a mere matter of "rewards." There are conditions to be met wherever we are. Life is for success. We have not lived if we have failed in our central undertaking. We have merely served an apprenticeship.

Success is adaptation to life as it comes to us from within. What makes life "worth while," as we say, is found through appreciation of the work given us to do, through response to our better nature. Success is never a mere game in which we get the better of our neighbor, whatever the world may assume on this point. Success is for higher self-realization. We have no rivals in the work we can do best. We feel dissatisfied simply because we have not yet accomplished our individual purpose—not because the world has failed us.

Sometimes indeed there is inward success in an undertaking accounted a failure by observers.

One may succeed in doing work for which one is not fitted, by sheer persistence in sticking to it. Some people wait many years before beginning their true work. Yet the real value of these secondary victories is seen in the use we make of the power acquired by meeting obstacles and then transferring our activities to some work that is to our liking. We may not judge merely by the vocation a man is now pursuing, by his profession, salary, profits, or even by his reputation in the community. For success involves the varied relationships of the inner life, and these are not apparent to the public eye. The man who knows himself understands what his work is doing for him, and how his life may be turned to higher account. We no longer praise people for mere resignation in accepting life's hardships and illnesses. We now look for the affirmative attitude.

Those of us who do fairly well in everything we undertake are deemed "lucky." But luck implies that there is a fortunate combination of circumstances more powerful than the man himself, who merely receives what comes, while others must work hard. Behind the scenes he who has really succeeded has been working as hard as anyone. The world often sees the finished result only, unaware of the years of incessant effort by which inner victories have been won and outward obstacles have been overcome. What we need to know is the inner history behind the alleged luck. There was an intelligible reason in every case, and no mere chance at all. There was alertness in meeting occasions, readiness in responding to opportunities which others did not take but might have taken. The man of character who "always lands on his feet" has acquired a certain art of rising to occasions. Then, too, we need to remind ourselves that there is Divine guidance prompting men from within, hence a spiritual law in events seemingly coming by chance.

Life offers us opportunities amidst law, order, system, and if we do not ignore or try to defeat life we move steadily forward. Life favors the man with true self-reliance. Life is for righteousness whatever sceptics may say to the contrary. Usually the one who complains that others are lucky is trying to force life to flow in some other channel. The pessimist would like to dictate terms to the universe. The optimist marvels at the order and beauty of things as they are.

This would be a mere platitude if men were not trying to get something for nothing. The time comes when people realize the great truth that every action brings its own reward, and that no one is excluded however unlucky he may seem to be. Then they learn that it is not true that "honesty is the best policy" because it "pays," but because honesty is right in itself. It is no longer a question of anything that simply "pays," but of that which preserves moral integrity and is right for all concerned. No mental device can secure for us a real sucess that is not deserved. What we need to make sure of in the first place is that we have something worth while to give the world. The more we have to give the less we need think of the reward that is coming to us.

In the world it is said of course that the conditions of life are hard, that one must live, and hence in the intense competition one is justified in adopting any method that may be in vogue. But this would not be success but surrender. To succeed we should expect to find a place and a work for ourselves, whatever the conditions. To surrender mentally is to weaken in life as a whole. But life calls for the affirmative attitude.

Some say that life is too short to succeed both in developing character and in earning a competency. Then let us decide in favor of character-building. But the saying is not true. The affirmative attitude strengthens us to believe that whatever is for us to do we will be able to do. We need not try to evade or put off anything that is right. Let us rather seek to live the truly complete life, regarding every apparent obstacle or handicap as an opportunity for success. We need not ask for more time or for favorable conditions. Time is ours and the conditions we need just now are at hand.

Success used to be judged by the amount of "push" with which an enterprise was launched. This type of activity was fostered by urging one's point at any cost, by clever advertising to create a demand, by seizing every opportunity to follow up an advantage to the limit. It was ingenious, competitive, often unscrupulous and disagreeably persistent. It could secure the sale of an inferior article. We all bought goods we did not want, before we understood the psychology of success. Now we know that the less value there is in a thing the more enterprise must be put into it to try to make us buy. It still "pays to advertise," but there are things that advertise themselves. It is a question of quality and of permanent value.

There is a sure road to success through honesty and steady persistence in right doing, with something to do for the world, or something to give to the world, even though results are not at once apparent. From this point of view financial rewards are signs but not the only evidences of success. There are many forms of moral success which bring no rewards in money at all, for instance, deeds of heroism in the case of a disaster at sea like the sinking of the *Titanic*. The true hero does not even ask for thanks, although he likes appreciation which shows insight into the law of service. Then, too, there is success by adaptation to nature in the case of explorations and discoveries. A part of the art of life consists in ability to meet changing conditions, all kinds of weather and hardships, when our work calls us into the various parts of the world. In a sense, adaptation to nature through the development of a sound mind and body, through due amount of exercise, rest, sleep and triumphant health is the basis of every other type of success.

Again, there is success through fidelity to friends, in the preservation of home-life at its best, the conservation of true marriage, fidelity to a high ideal of love and truth and of a great cause. All such successes are measured by their own invisible rewards. Only he who gives abundantly receives in large measure. These successes become ends in themselves, while our external life is regarded as means only or as secondary.

If all worthy successes contribute to what we call spiritual success, let us agree that resignation is not in any sense the ideal. Not by mere self-effacement or self-sacrifice can we give our best to the world. What we need is strong belief in the triumph of the right, the beautiful, the true, together with consecration to do our part, to devote ourselves to our work. It is not a question of what we give up but of what we manifest. The more fully we give ourselves in the direction in which we can give best, the more we shall possess of the joys and opportunities which stand for fulness of life.

To start with the idea of God as all-encompassing Spirit, with the universe regarded as existing for spiritual ends, is to accord spiritual things the first rank from beginning to end, hence to see that spiritual success is the one real success. As spirits we have a two-fold relationship, one in the spiritual world to the more direct activities of the Divine life; and one in the natural world where as dwellers in the flesh we take on the conditions that come to us by birth. It is on the Divine side that we draw from the great resources which bring success over external obstacles. What seems impossible outwardly becomes possible from within.

We have the power of the Spirit within us to rise above circumstances through insight into their meaning for the soul. The whole life-situation is changed for us when we grasp the inner point of view. We then see the spiritual transforming and expressing itself through the natural. What once seemed a hardship now proves to be an opportunity. Our external conditions prove adverse only so long as we regard them negatively. True success always grows out of the affirmative attitude. True success is for the individual and for society at the same time. There is no conflict ultimately speaking between self-realization and service. For true success is based on the higher truth of man's being. It implies the inspiring idea that there is but one Power in the universe and that this power is manifested in a world-order which makes for spiritual success.

XVI

INSTANTANEOUS HEALING

MANY years ago Dr. Quimby remarked that the time would come when people would once more be healed by word of mouth as in the case of the remarkable healings wrought by Jesus and the apostles. How is such healing possible and when may we expect "the greater works" promised by the Master?

At first thought the prospect of instantaneous healing seems incredible if not utterly impossible. This is probably the reason which led devotees of the church to classify scriptural healing as miraculous. Apparently there is no way by which a person can suddenly be lifted from a well-nigh hopeless state of disease, especially if it comes on gradually out of cumulative causes; for we know that time is required for recovery in case of diseases of long standing. There seems to be no way of ridding the human system of its disorders except through a regular series of changes.

If, however, we examine the scriptural record to learn what we can about the works of healing, we find that there is a certain resemblance in the several instances which affords us a clue. So far as the record informs us the works of healing were wrought among the "common people," who heard the Master gladly. Such people, we know from acquaintance with them today, have greater emotional responsiveness, greater powers of self-abandonment, than the socially elect and the learned possess. These come by their maladies more quickly, and whatever they yield they let go of more readily. They are, therefore, able to give themselves with more implicit faith to any power or any person inspiring faith. It is wholly credible that people of this responsive type should so have given themselves in faith to the Master as to have been made suddenly "whole."

Such healing would, let us say, lift the spirit of the sometime sufferer to a higher level of consciousness with such power, with such an impetus that a new mode of life would result, as in the case of those remarkable conversions which still occur from time to time through missionary work in the slums of a great city. This changed centre of equilibrium would bring its attendant consequences and make the cure complete so far as it could be wrought by another. The subsequent results would depend upon the intelligence of the individual in living the new mode of life thoughtfully.

From the point of view of the therapeutist, instantaneous healing would result from penetrating insight into the real state of soul, the true inner life of the patient. This insight would be accompanied by power to make it good. The keener the insight, the more sharp would be the separation made through the Christ-consciousness between the spirit of the patient and his former malady. The patient would not only receive the benefit of the display of healing power, but hear such a thrilling word as "Thy faith hath made thee whole," "Take up thy bed and walk." The Christ would both act and speak "as one having authority."

Dr. Quimby used to say that "the explanation is the cure." By this he meant the penetrating truth which struck home and touched the real cause of disease, whatever appearances might be. Strictly speaking, the cure was wrought by that insight, and if the patient grasped it, the cure was immediate, so far as the inner life was concerned. For we either see a thing or we do not. What leads up to it is preliminary. When the insight really comes, nothing more need be said. Hence Quimby very suddenly and convincingly spoke to some of his patients that illuminating word which carried the most far-reaching results, results affecting not only the health but the religion, business, mode of life and happiness of the patient. With the growth of this power of discernment, Quimby found himself able to speak the healing word more effectively. Hence, he foresaw the time when the clarifying word would itself be sufficient.

We have all on occasion made inner changes as quickly as that. For example, a man sees that he has been a fool, and in detecting his folly grasps in an instant the cause of much trouble and as quickly drops his trouble with all its side issues. A person realizes in a flash that he has been duped and in the same flash utterly changes his attitude toward the people and things involved. Thus in a moment of electrifying self-consciousness, a young person who has been infatuated realizes his predicament. The "affair" is all over at once. There is nothing more to say. It would be utterly out of the question to pretend to love the other partner to the experience. As quickly, also, a commercial deal may come to an end.

Granted truth-seeking and truth-telling people enough in the world, people would be taken out of their hypocrisies and pretensions right and left. Nothing is so swift in its effect as truth. The only difficulty in the world in this regard is that truth is not welcome. If we encouraged the man of insight, it would become customary for people to cure one another of their errors and conceits, to say nothing of what are called their "sins."

We may expect the greater works promised by the Master when people more seriously adopt the healing principle which goes straight to the heart, down to the very foundation of human life. As of old, those who are responsive in type will give themselves most readily to such healing. But there is hope for us all. Ideally speaking, it is possible that a word should be spoken to any one of us which would take us immediately out of our darkness. When we see the light, the rest follows.

Many of the instances of spontaneous healing of which we hear from time to time are instantaneous in type. A bedridden invalid may suddenly do the impossible when a threatening fire breaks out and there is no one at hand to help. This happened in the case of one who rose from her bed, packed her trunk and dragged it down four flights of stairs to a place of safety, suffering no relapse. It sometimes happens when a physician or some member of the family despairingly resorts to a trick in order to arouse the bedridden creatures of habits to help themselves. If a shock may kill, a shock can also cure. What some people need is the equivalent of a shock.

But spiritual healing will become more intelligent as we proceed, and it will no longer be necessary to shock people into activity. That is to say, the sick and the sorrowing will be more quickly restored if they so will. There are always people who refuse to look at the truth as long as they are able to be evasive. Many could be cured quickly enough now if they wished to be. But people either avoid the effort or the direct view which discloses their inward self in all the actuality of concealed motives and intentions.

Death is probably an instantaneous healing for many people, or rather the process of coming to judgment which follows it when there is no longer any way to hide from oneself. Some of us would prefer to look reality straight in the eye here and now. There is marvelous help, there are unbounded resources for those who are ready to give themselves in full confidence to the Spirit. We might even be raised suddenly from a state of "spiritual death" into one of hearty responsiveness to the Life whose resources are infinite. It is not a question of the length of time the soul has lain in the tomb of carnal consciousness, but of the summoning power of the Christ. "Lazarus, come forth," "Maiden, I say unto thee, arise!" is the great word.

Someone has said that the only healing is self-healing. This is true if by such healing we mean the dawning in our own consciousness of the truth which has set us free, the awareness of that

Life to which we owe our restoration. So, too, a conversion or any other spiritual change becomes truly ours when we see it, and, touched to the quick, will to make the new life our own.

In a more profound sense, it might be said that the only genuine healing is the cure of our selfishness. Other healings are introductory. It is surely within our power to turn abruptly from our selfishness within a single day, in an hour, a moment. We do not even need to wait for a quickening vision like that which came to Saul on the road to Damascus and made him, by his consent, Paul, the greatest of apostles; for we have much more enlightenment now. The world now sees with crystal clearness that selfishness is the one great trouble. Then, too, there are countless aids at hand if one wills to become unselfish. We need not stop to plead, to ask for reasons and await results. As suddenly as an apparently obscure private may become a hero at the front by venturing to do the brave deed at which his comrades hesitate, so any one of us might step forth a new man; for either "we have the mind of Christ" or this transfiguring mind is close at hand in the person of someone who will manifest it in our presence. The response made to us by the Christ is never limited. "Be thou made clean." "According to thy faith be it unto thee."

XVII

THE OVERCOMING OF DISEASE

THE question is often asked why it is that a man in perfect physical health may be taken suddenly ill and die a few days after, although under the most skilful medical care. Here, for example, is an exceptionally strong man in the prime of life, engaged in a congenial occupation, one that is not too taxing and is likely to sustain his good health instead of militating against it. He is a highly educated man, with well-trained powers and an uncommonly acute intellect. Moreover, he is philosophically inclined and seems to be wiser in his attitude toward life than most men. His special interest is also favorable to wisdom in daily living. Apparently everything is in his favor. Yet when the disease seizes him he rapidly collapses and his physicians soon announce that there is no hope. He passes out of this life even more rapidly than men with far less strength and much less intellectual power.

Of course death in such a case may be the simple result of medical ignorance and practice. Powerful remedies may be put into his system

to excess, nervousness, excitement or tension; and that this nervous excess is in turn due to some activity which he has been overdoing, without giving his spirit sufficient time to overcome the daily fatigue. Thus thinking, he knows that the outward excess may be overcome by lifting his consciousness to a higher level, becoming inwardly still, breaking connection with the lower level of disturbances. The spirit in fact may calm the disturbances as a wisely calm person might quell a mob by enunciating a great truth which clears away all misconceptions and undermines the hot-headedness. The spirit may go further on occasion, that is, may direct the therapeutic power straight to the disturbed region and bring about a remarkable change in a few minutes.

For interior peace or spiritual poise in the sense in which we are here using the term is power-inviting or dynamic in unusual degree. To regain it by lifting the spirit into unison with the Divine presence is to change the centre of equilibrium, the basis of activity. When peace ensues where excitement might have reigned, when repose is in control and consciousness is absorbed in spiritual realization, the mind as a whole not only becomes favorable but is put into a state to shift the balance of power throughout the organism. This accomplished, the temperature begins to go down, the heart and lungs resume their normal rhythms, and other consequences follow as matters of course. It is not necessary to keep up the inner process or realization. For the crisis is past; as we say, the tide has been turned. The same disturbance which might have been developed into a severe or fatal illness is by the right interpretation and the right action, at "the psychological moment," turned into a relatively trivial series of states which soon pass away of their own volition.

If the person who thus conquers the inceptive stages of illness, by turning them into something trivial, learns a lesson from the experience he may presently take a further step, that is, by avoiding the excess, whatever it may have been, which brought on the initial disturbance. Such a one is likely to regard all painful sensations as incidental and to put the most favorable interpretation upon them. After a while it becomes a question, not of the mere overcoming of an illness, but of a regular mode of life tending to bring health as a consequence without any thought of disease.

Every person has a way of meeting life. Some of us are highly emotional and readily enter into a disturbing experience in such a way as to drain the nervous forces. Nearly all emotions are exhausting, and angry emotions use up the nerve-energy with remarkable rapidity. To see that this is true in one's own case and to profit by it is to make ready to cultivate those other mental qualities, such as calmness and moderation of thought, which give strength. Going further still, one learns the true or spiritual source of calmness and strength, and cultivates that mode of life which is devoid of all emotional excess. Worthy emotions may still find place, but all worthy emotion is tempered by wisdom or moderation.

Whatever the temperament, the great point to gain is willingness to make the venture, to turn from a disturbance to the realm of higher and finer power within. To unite with that Power, declaring "I am spirit and have infinite Life to draw upon," or whatever the realization may be, is to break with the disturbing element, turn the tide. If one must put some sort of interpretation upon the disturbance in order to be at rest, let it be called a process of cleansing or readjustment. Or call it simply "progress." For it should not be regarded as a condition taken on from the outside. In the natural order of things we become aware of a disturbance when something foreign is being brought to the surface and cast off, just as we become unpleasantly self-conscious when a trait of character is undergoing change. To regard the process as incidental and promising, is to put oneself in line with it, that is, in line with the creative Life behind it. Our part is to unite with this Life, not to dwell upon the process. Therefore our realization should always be such as to make this union the more secure. The vital point is that a disturbance which might be developed into a disease if met according to the old order of thought, is given exactly the opposite turn by realizing the truth which is "the cure." Wonderful to relate, an apparently threatening illness may pass off in a few minutes, simply by giving the whole experience the right turn at the right time for making as little of it as possible.

Too much emphasis cannot be placed on the importance of rightly interpreting our sensations and pains. This in fact is the vital point with most of us. And at this point we find enlightened medical opinion in our day in line with the conclusions of the spiritual healer. Dr. Richard Cabot emphasizes, for example, the importance of taking account of the high degree of suggestibility to which so many people are subject.[1] Three examples of such suggestibility are cited: misinterpretation of sensations which might indicate heart disease, cancer or insanity. "People are amazingly prone to fancy that they have heart disease. If they have any symptoms in that part of the body where they are taught to believe that the heart resides, or especially if they

[1] "Social Work," p. 93.

know someone who has recently died of heart disease, there are many people likely first to believe that they have heart trouble, and then to have actual symptoms which they attribute to heart disease." Insanity is feared far more often. Cancer is the most dreaded of all diseases, "but one of the most unnecessarily feared," inasmuch as the only alleged basis for it may be "trifling pains or stomach troubles, troubles that all of us would disregard." In the same way a person will speak of a "pain across the kidneys" when the kidneys are perfectly healthy. Again, a man will think that he has this or that disease when all that troubles him is a "tired stomach." Fatigue of the eyes is also very common and very misleading.

If, then, we would overcome disease from within we must begin by learning how to interpret our pains aright. Many a potential disease is dismissed in a quiet sort of way without any malady at all by the man who knows how to give his sensations the right turn at the right moment. For the wise man makes as little as he can of his ills. Turning them off as incidental, he refuses to name them, refuses to associate them with conventional fears. It is then a question of a quiet rest for a day or so, or of silent spiritual help enlisted at the appropriate moment. If the stomach is tired, then the stomach is given a rest, and no fears are entertained concerning the kidneys. If the eyes are tired, rest for the eyes is sought. Always there is discrimination between pain and the interpretation put upon it.

Furthermore, one who is wise in this direction bears in mind the further fact stated by Dr. Cabot, namely, that "the vast majority of diseases get well without any help from anybody." Since this is the case, why name them in the first place? Why run to the doctor? Why accept the notion that disease is cured by medicine instead of being cured by the resident forces within the individual? If most maladies tend to run themselves out any way, while others can be "starved out" and some will disappear if we keep quiet and rest, 'why make so much of disease? Why not emphasize health and the way to attain and keep it?

Plainly, all these are individual matters. It is for each man to learn the difference between his own pains and his own interpretations of them, his suggestibility, his dependence on medical or other opinion, bondage to fear. Most of our fears are borrowed. They go with some medical or religious belief which we have accepted—without much thought. They have little basis in fact. It is mere matter of common sense, therefore, to face them, face the worst and see how far we are from it, how slight is the foundation of our misery.

What we need is courage to make the venture in the spiritual direction. What had always seemed impossible may easily come within our power, when we plunge in and make a beginning by taking our spiritual faith seriously. And when we have dismissed our temporary or superficial ills, the way will be open to face the real problems of spiritual healing.

XVIII

CREATIVE HEALTH

HEALTH is usually regarded as an end in itself, to be sought directly, as we might go out in quest of pleasure. Hence people have in the past consulted physicians and have taken medicines and drugs simply to be relieved of their aches and pains. So, too, people have more recently visited mental healers, insisting that what they wanted was health; they did not care to hear a word concerning the spiritual life. Most of us who have had to give special attention to our health have been inclined to regard it as a distinct possession, a state of the body to be gained without much regard to the state of the mind or spirit. We have had to learn from experience that health as a true possession is inseparably connected with the mode of life we live.

Meanwhile, instances have been observed in which health has been restored to people who have given up the quest for it as a distinct end, and have, fortunately for them, yielded their minds to other interests. Health has, for example, come to men and women who have deserved it by giving themselves in full consecration to their life-work in the world. Any experience which thus brings health as a sort of by-product is instructive because it suggests that health might best be sought by first pursuing a higher end, by doing one's true work as leader, scholar, artist, as a productive agent of any kind. Health might therefore be regarded as creative. By this term, "creative health," one therefore means that larger health which springs from the life or conduct which is most intimately characteristic of the individual.

The Englishman who, doomed by the verdict of his physicians, to die within six months, entirely regained his health by first asking how he could most fully enjoy life during the time that remained to him, merely exemplified this principle in part. Exceedingly fond of hunting and fishing, this man gave himself up to the sheer pleasure of life in the open without thinking of any result that might come to him. Despite the possibility of catching cold in the swamps and in stormy weather, he indulged in all sorts of exposure to the elements without fear and without resistance. Nature doubtless relieved him of many a tension and inner obstruction because he yielded his organism unqualifiedly, inasmuch as he expected to die whatever he did. So nature might be kind to us all if we would do our part in full responsiveness, anticipating only benefits. Men have sometimes built up a rugged constitution through life in the open, or in contact with real hardship through constant exposure as in war-time, when their main interest was far removed from the pursuit of health. It is not recorded, however, that many who merely sought their own pleasure through exposure to nature have helped their fellow men to gain the vision of creative health.

Another man, very different in type from the Englishman and beset by headaches which no one could overcome for him, resolved to try the experiment of benefiting his head by using it to the limit, a heroic remedy most of us would say. Taking up an intellectual investigation with steady persistence, this courageous worker became sound in mind and body by using his powers instead of letting them lie fallow while seeking material aids. In so doing he found his vocation once for all in a field of original research which enlisted his intellect to the full. Undoubtedly his energies were pent-up prior to the discovery of this productive outlet. His motive in becoming a scholar may not have been philanthropic, but he surely found himself by losing himself in his work.

More inspiring by far was the case of a woman who, like the Englishman who loved to hunt and fish, was limited by the best physicians of her time to six months more in this natural world. Her question was not, How may I have the best time in six months remaining to me? but, How may I do most for my fellow men in this short time? Remembering that in the slums of the city in which she lived there was a house belonging to her family, she asked leave to dedicate this house to social service for the benefit of the poor and needy. Taking the house into her charge and becoming absorbed in the opportunities which contact with the laboring classes brought her, this deep lover of good works found the allotted six months passing into the years, and the years bringing her a state of health which could be prolonged into the fulness of life. She, too, not only found her vocation but in such a way that many co-workers were stimulated into creative activity by her example. Health did not at once cease to be a goal to be kept in sight, but it became a secondary good to be guarded for the sake of a life rich in opportunities for service. Her health came unsought when there was no apparent hope that she could survive beyond six months. This health was in brief a gift of her spiritual life. It came as an added element, not as a possession which seemed within human power to bestow. What resulted in her life might come in full many an instance if with equal zeal men and women who have no hope in material things were to give themselves as resolutely to some work supremely worth while. Thus creative work in any field might produce that wonderful health which is of the Spirit.

In a measure this was the kind of health which Dr. Quimby's labors produced for him when, ostensibly a mere student of mental influences and in dire need of health, he undertook the investigations which led to the modern discovery of spiritual healing.[1] Dr. Quimby apparently had but a short time to live. Yet he completely regained his health while scarcely thinking about it. While studying the phenomena of what we now call "suggestion" and the subconscious, he found a vocation of absorbing interest. His first interests could hardly have been called spiritual at all, although there may have been a Divine purpose that he should discover the silent method of healing at that time. He was not looking for light upon his own health when it dawned upon him with such fulness. There appeared to be little left to create health out of, so far as his physical condition was concerned. There was no one at hand to tell him to seek his freedom by spiritual means, unless we say that the Spirit within him taught him to look beyond material forces. But by discerning laws of mind which

1 "A History of the New Thought Movement," Chap. II.

he could utilize to set people free from bondage to mere opinion and teach them a true "Science of Health" he became filled with the life-interest which brought his own spiritual health and with it his bodily health.[1]

According to the principles which Dr. Quimby was thereby led to adopt, health is the natural right of every human soul. The presence of the Creator with us through the wisdom which guides and the love which sustains is for the sake of health, among ends of greater value than health itself. We ought therefore to judge by what God is endeavoring to quicken in us and produce through us, taking the whole of our life into account. We ought not to judge by physical signs or symptoms. We should judge by the immanent Life which makes for rounded development. Taking this as our clue, it should not seem strange at all that a person may find his health spiritually by discovering his work in the world. In Quimby's case the work and the health were apparently one and the same. His theory that health is a consequence of understanding and rightly using our powers grew out of his own quests. He created his own health, if you please, by discovering a new field of service. But in the larger sense God created these gifts through

[1] "The Quimby Manuscripts," Chap. III.

him. Man's extremity was once more God's opportunity.

Quimby's patients were in large measure in the same position. They had no hope physically. They had not found themselves or found their work. This was as true of Mrs. Patterson (later Mrs. Eddy) as of Rev. Mr. Evans, who became the first writer on the subject, and of the other pioneers. Coming simply to be restored to health, if his work as a "last resort" could save them, they found not merely health but a work to do in leading others into the same freedom. Quimby was their forerunner or guide. He could save and cure in so far as anyone, divinely guided, may rescue another from the borders of the grave and give a new lease of life. Yet there was still a work to be done, namely, their own creative response through the discovery of the greater self and its field for individual service. This meant that each one who became a pioneer in the new work of freeing the soul must think out the central principles concerning the Christ as the true healing power. The individual need afforded the special problem for each to solve, that he might prove the truth of Quimby's teaching for himself. He might have little capital as it were to begin with: it was for him to aid in the process of creating health by means of this small beginning.

When, for example, a patient came to Quimby whose inner life was suppressed, with the nervous energies pent-up and causing trouble, the function of the silent spiritual treatment was to touch the dormant life into action and start the soul on its way to freedom. Through the intuition which came to Quimby to meet the individual's needs, he did that work for another which the sufferer was unable to do for himself. It then remained for the sometime sufferer to come into spiritual understanding, that he might learn what conditions had caused his trouble and how to live so that such conditions need never recur. Thus a patient who had been an invalid for six years as a result of over-study in school, in gaining her health learned how to use her sensitive disposition and exceptional intuitive powers for the benefit of others beset by similar conditions. Thus the young man whom we have spoken of in Chapter I found himself as a true follower of Christ. The greatest work wrought by Quimby may therefore rightfully be called creative.

Yet in these and all cases where striking results ensued, where there was a life of service continuing throughout the years that followed, the healing was only the beginning of the creative work. The healing gave the impetus which when followed with constancy of faith enabled the individual to enter in and take possession of the benefits produced in the inner life. These became permanent with the discovery of the power to go to the same Divine sources. To find these sources was to discover the inner Word, to begin to read the eternal Word as the book of the soul's progress.

Now, the individual who thus began to find the priceless possession may not have been wholly restored to health when this regeneration began. He may not have reached the point where he was free from bodily ills and able to demonstrate the spiritual law on all occasions. That is not the crucial point. Many take up their public work before they are wholly free. The point is that the remaining conditions offer the resistance needed to enable a person to attain creative health. These are the conditions one must master for oneself. They are there to test the soul. They are incentives to productive action. It is much more than a question of "the besetting sin." Say rather that it is the understanding and mastering of disposition or temperament, and the perfecting of character through Divine help. Through the individual's victory the same forces which apparently made for disease are now turned into account in favor of health so that they make for freedom. Thus the hardships of a sensitive disposition, misunderstood, become the benefits of the same disposition brought into constructive play.

Many have wondered why greater results have not been achieved through mental healing. They have wondered too why there has sometimes been a return of former troubles and maladies, and why some patients have not been restored at all. Here is a prime reason. This greater work is spiritual. It comes from Divine wisdom. No merely mental therapeutist can ever bestow it upon another, although abundantly able to overcome superficial ills. It begins with that quickening of the soul which shows that only through inner regeneration is the individual brought into the living abundance known as creative health.

It may well be that some are started on their way unwittingly, as in the case of those who found their health by forgetting themselves in a life of service. But we are saying that the greater step is into the spiritual knowledge which shows how the change is wrought, how health can become creatively permanent. In the same way others are started on the road by the use of denials and affirmations, without realizing that there is a more intelligent method. But the great consideration is change from mental methods to interior awareness that there is an influx of Life which is the constant source of health. It is knowledge of this influent Life which lifts the whole restorative process and makes it creative. From this influx when known as guidance there comes the impetus to do one's greatest work in the world. Hence the whole pursuit of health changes into quest for the larger spiritual life.

To put matters this way is to pass beyond former ideas concerning salvation and the acknowledgment of sin. These are implied, to be sure. A man must see with open eye what his selfishness was and what misery it caused. He must trace matters to his own self-love, must will to reform in order that the regenerative process may begin in earnest. Yet merely to be "saved" is little indeed in comparison with what the modern world understands by the life through which a man is asked to prove by his works that he is saved. Real regeneration begins to show itself when life becomes constructive.

Thus Saul, the sometime persecutor of the new faith taught by Jesus, became Paul the great apostle of the doctrine he once opposed. We are no longer concerned with what he was before his quickening came, but with the quickening impetus which brought him "the mind of Christ."

What might be accomplished if we should work first and last for these conditions which inspire creative health? Few of us know, because we are not yet quickened in this spiritually constructive way. We still dwell on human woe and misery, condemning people for their sin and looking upon evil as a mystery. We still lament that no quick road to health is found for all. We still talk about doctrines as if they possessed magic power to save the soul. In our schools we still educate for the intellectual life, instead of training the young to make ready for the fulness of life.

What if we were to seek directly that spiritual life which not only makes for permanent health but discloses the purpose for which we live? What if we should begin forthwith by doing this work which God calls us to do, whether it seems to make for health or not? This would be adopting in entire seriousness the promise that Christ came to bring the abundant life. It would imply firm belief in the spiritual law, namely, that we should first seek the kingdom of God and the righteousness pertaining to the kingdom before going in quest of the things which are to be added. It would be putting health on the spiritual basis, as a gift of the Spirit.

XIX

THE SECRET PLACE

LOOKING back over the ground we have attained in the preceding chapters, we realize that while in spirit those who believe in healing by the Christ-method may be in accord, their understanding of the method and the process may be very different. If we begin by declaring that the real self is never disturbed in spirit but ever remains true to the image and likeness of God, it would seem plain that the one course to pursue is to break from any impeding consciousness, affirm that the self is in perfect peace and health, and deny any alleged trouble. This is the simple method by which many have helped themselves and others. This process seems so successful that the tendency is to put all matters in the present tense, to claim as already true everything we aspire to be and will to realize. Hence it has become matter of habit with many to choose new affirmations for each week or month but always to phrase them as if the ideals they suggest were realized now.

On the other hand, if we agree that our

troubles and diseases regarded in the light of their relation to character and the soul's welfare have spiritual causes which must be acknowledged and removed, to deny might be to gloss over and to procrastinate. Healing does not pass beyond the merely mental plane and become spiritual until it has to do with our real attitude or prevailing love. Morally speaking, there is no substitute for coming to judgment in utter sincerity. What we need is to see the self and see it whole, with open eye. This self is indeed the spirit whose perfection we constantly affirm. This self is always a child of God, in His image and likeness, untouched in the inmost region. Yet why should we ever have reason to affirm its sanctity or deny the power of any influence to thwart it unless there were a problem needing solution and a difficulty to be overcome?

It would seem well then to pass from the affirmative to the intuitive method as soon as we can, and begin thorough study of the hidden self. From the heights of theoretical affirmation there is bound to be a fall sooner or later. Why not come down as quickly as possible and adopt the attitude and the pace which we can maintain throughout the years? Surely we must do this if we are to pass beyond interest in merely mental health and healing to spiritual health and healing. It will then become a question of that greater truth of the Christ-spirit which sets men permanently free.

Moreover, if we accept the idea of the Divine presence as an influx tending to produce changes calling for co-operation on our part from stage to stage, we must admit that much still remains to be attained. We not only do not find people possessing the open vision in large degree, responsive in mind and body to the tide of the Spirit, but very few indeed who even have the idea of any such relationship. To gain an insight into this glorious possibility is to realize that one could hardly claim to possess such union with God unless one were to pretend to be the Christ in fulness. Instead of any sort of claim there is a prayer that, having had a glimpse of what this union may be, one may be progressively led into it.

To endeavor to move forward with the influent Life, in order to give that Life full and free expression, bringing mind and body into line stage by stage, is to be prepared in the first place to learn everything one can from any source concerning the present obstructions, that one may see where to begin. What we ought to know is the present or actual state of development, the needs just now at hand, together with the wisdom to meet those needs and see the way to take the next step in spiritual evolution. To discover these needs one must be in the attitude of frank acknowledgment, of willingness to learn and to be led. Thus one adopts the view that there is such a wealth of wisdom to be disclosed to us that it can only be given progressively.

At the same time there is that other aspect of the truth, namely, that the self already is potentially what it presently becomes in actual expression, so that all growth is realization. If we place too much stress on the affirmation of "our oneness with God," we tend to lose sight of the soul's progress through changing conditions from lower to higher. But if we put too much emphasis on the conditions, we lose sight of the ideal. There is a point of view which includes these two truths. "So build we up the being that we are," says the poet. All progress is realization. Yet the conditions of growth are no less necessary. The hidden self already is what it would be. We cannot make the self over. We cannot reform our neighbors. In a sense the self never changes. Yet only through change does life continue.

There is, in short, a course which the incoming Life takes through us in its age-long revelation of eternal truth and its continuous creation of the human spirit into perfection. What we need is a way of thinking which is faithful to actual experience as a progressive revelation, and a method of response to the Spirit which makes us mindful of our present opportunities. We shall not be bound or limited by present conditions if we regard these as means which the Spirit takes to its high end.

It is easy to lapse into the idea that the process of life through which we are passing is itself the whole reality. To break from this tendency we need a way to lift the spirit into renewed vision of the ideal. Hence we need to remind ourselves again and again that there is a secret place within the soul where we may always commune with God. Our sometime absorption in processes and conditions need never be taken to imply that the whole spirit is absorbed. Hence we may dwell for the time being on that other half of the truth that is too great for words, namely, that in spirit we are never disturbed, however great our alienation in consciousness from the Father.

It is never given us in our imperfect human speech to say precisely where God in wise and loving presence with us ceases, where man in his uplift of heart and will begins. But what language cannot directly say a scriptural passage may impressively suggest. Hence we say to ourselves, as if speaking for that Presence: "Be still, and know that I am God," endeavoring to be genuinely still as we repeat the passage: "Thou wilt keep him in perfect peace whose mind is stayed on Thee, because he trusteth in Thee." "He that dwelleth in the secret place of the Most High shall abide under the shadow of the Almighty." These sayings bring us into the secret place *as an experience,* and that is what we need.

When we are in need of help we naturally concentrate upon the ideal, reminding ourselves that despite any appearance there is an inmost region of the spirit which remains untouched, in intimate relation with the heavenly influx. This is the side of our nature we wish to concentrate upon to gain a fresh impetus to turn once more to the experience of meeting the obstacles that lie in our path. When we turn toward the secret place in thought, we realize that with the overcoming of friction at the centre there will be a change throughout the organism. Hence we desire that touch with the renewing Life which shall send a thrill throughout our being comparable to that which comes when we are deeply touched by familiar music after having been long deprived of it. In the moment of detaching our consciousness from outward things to renew the ideal in the secret place, we may well yield ourselves to the experience as if nothing else were true, as if nothing else existed.

To avoid the pitfalls of self-absorption and abstraction in which some find themselves at this point, we need a clearer way of thinking about the human spirit or self in contrast with the mind and the body. By the human spirit we mean both the immortal part of us, the soul or son of God created in His image and likeness, already dwelling in the spiritual world, and the being who is conscious and self-conscious in the successive phases of natural existence. That is to say, the spirit potentially is far nobler in quality and greater in power than in any actual experience we yet know. The spirit is in part an ideal or purpose. But the spirit is also the self or soul already aware of an ideal in contrast with the conditions of life round about us in the natural world. The spirit is the distinctive individual, the permanent identity or ego surviving any sort of change. Yet we are learning to know ourselves here in this world through changes. The human spirit in ideal is one, is a consistent harmony of all its elements or qualities enduring through any vicissitudes. Yet in present experience we find ourselves far from this unity.

It is untrue to declare, as some affirm, that whatever is true of God as Infinite Spirit is true of us as finite spirits; for God as infinite, uncreated, is all-encompassing Life, while we are recipients, each with his place and his gifts. The secret place is not the point of "blending" but the region where we may attain adjustment and unison leading to co-operation, God and man remaining distinct. The secret place is a sphere of attainment, not of relapse, resignation or absorption. It would have no meaning for us at all unless it disclosed to us "the flying perfect" ever leading us on toward the goal of social realization which we call the kingdom of heaven. Forth from our renewed experience of the ideal there ought always to proceed clearer thinking, as we turn from spirit to mind, from mind to body.

By the term "mind" we mean the whole complexity and variety of activities taking place within us, from sensation to intuition in its highest moments. We mean, further, the different levels or planes of consciousness, the differences between inner and outer conditions, interior and exterior states, the subjective and the objective, and all those contrasts which we know as duality of self or conflict of voices. The mind is in close relation with the brain and through the brain with the whole body. But the spirit's most intimate relation is with God, without whose constant presence there would not be one moment of being.

When we try to give full meaning to the intermediate term "mind," hence by contrast to know the secret places of the spirit, it is helpful to make the transition in thought from outward things to the inmost sanctuary.[1] The starting-point of the mind in this process is with sensation. Sensa-

[1] See also "The Open Vision," p. 140.

tions give us "things," with color, light, heat, sound, touch, and the rest. Then come emotions and feelings associating themselves with sensation, such as fear or pleasure. Desires arise, too, in this association with things around us in the world. By "will" we mean the more interior element of our mental life through which we select between desires, eliminating some, overcoming and using others, and transfiguring those that are most eligible. Will possesses a freedom which desires could never have, hence will springs from within and at its best expresses the heart. Then, too, there is thought, the intellect or understanding. What we will to do and to be depends not alone upon the selection between desires but upon analysis, interpretation, and reasoning. All these qualities of our inner life pertain to "mind."

What is it that possesses mind, that feels, thinks and wills? The human spirit. When does the spirit act from within in contrast with its responsiveness to interests from without? When it possesses "the understanding heart." The spirit thinks and wills from within when it thinks from enlightenment and from the Divine love. The various mental elements whereby the spirit expresses itself in action then become like obedient servants doing the will of a wise master. The spirit is the real master. Mind might be a faithful servant in each of us if we understood and had learned to control all the mental elements. It is the spirit that controls. It is the mind that is brought into order.

So far each of us may confirm the description by experience. By "the secret place" we mean something more than the self-consciousness which shows us the difference between mind and spirit. For self-consciousness, we know, is often an interference, and when we would be receptive we try too hard to be still, or permit our thought to suggest too many ideas. Consciousness does not follow into the secret place to tell us just when God is present there with His guiding wisdom and sustaining love. But consciousness does yield the great contrast between our lesser and our larger moments.

What figure of speech shall we choose to express the ineffable union of God and man in the secret place? Let us keep to the imagery which the term "life" suggests. Life, we know, moves forward, brings changes. Its inflow is like that of a stream with its current and its waves or rhythms. It moves harmoniously in a ready channel. It struggles against any obstacle. If impeded, its flow is affected by the obstacle, often seriously so.

Far more truly than in the case of a river impeded by obstructions in its course, the life-current within us depends upon our response. The secret place in the inmost of the spirit is the region of intimate relationship between guiding life and recipient soul, ready or not to be guided as the case may be. Life comes as pure essence. It is received by the heart through affection and will as love. It is then received by the understanding as light. The understanding heart is quickened by heavenly love and wisdom. Thus quickened in willingness to be guided, responding to love as Divine, to wisdom as Divine, taking no credit to itself, the human spirit is prompted from within in the secret place, and the understanding "thinks with the spirit" instead of thinking merely with the brain. The whole inner life may then be prompted from the secret place, mind as a whole may respond, and the brain as a whole will become obedient.

Sometimes this relationship of God and man is thought of merely in the light of receptivity. But as important as receptivity may be, it is only the beginning. The secret place is indeed the place of worship, the place for listening, waiting humility. Our help is indeed solely in the Lord. Yet we have our whole mental life to bring into play, and unless we enlist thought and will, feeling and the sense of effort in activities springing from the Lord these mental elements will find some other outlet. The spirit is not alone a recipient of Life but also able to assimilate and co-operate.

The secret place is the place for beginning to do things. Our great need is to return there for fresh quickening, a new touch with Life, then outgoing activity expressing Life in our human activities. It is the place of conjunction between the Divine and the human. The ideal of this union is the Divine-human, the Christ. The place is the region of the incarnation of the heavenly Heart in the human heart.

Incarnation means, for the individual, response according to need, purpose and capacity, leading to concrete or practical action. We are most likely to be quickened in large measure by an individual need when we seek the quietude of the secret place in order to serve another. We are uplifted by the idea of the Divine purpose for us when we realize that through the secret place we may be led to act more wisely than we know, may be led to do just our work in the world. That it is a question of capacity we see clearly when we note how greatly individuals differ in talents or gifts. What our own capacity for receiving may be we never learn save so far as we pass far beyond receptivity to effective expression. What the Divine purpose is for us we learn in large part by experience, not by theorizing. What we most need we ourselves seldom know, but we may seek the inner silence in readiness to be filled according to need.

Humility is a word seldom used nowadays by those who have reacted against the old theology. It seems now to be solely a question of self-reliance and self-realization. Yet something like humility we always need when likely to express self-love, pride, mere learning or self-righteousness. There will always be tendencies into side issues and temptations so long as we are human. Humility is the corrective of self-assertiveness. One might under-estimate the self, hence fail to stand upright in the secret place. But most of us are likely to err the other way.

What we need above all, on the human side, is enlightenment to the effect that there is a movement of Life outward from the secret place into the understanding or intellectual life, hence throughout the mind and into the body. We need to think of life as *dynamic,* with us to *achieve* and to achieve with energy. We need to think of this dynamic Life as achieving by taking a certain direction, pursuing an end. Our part is very far from merely passive adjustment. Our part is responsive movement forward *with Life.* Life is creative. So must our response be.

In our ordinary thinking we are apt to limit creative genius to the poet, composer or sculptor, that is, to the lover of Beauty. But far more truly the lover of Truth is a creative recipient of Life. The Spirit is with us to attain creative expression through us in behalf of Beauty, Truth, and Goodness, the eternal Ideas. These are the three great ends. There is one Spirit with diversity of gifts making toward the eternal values or ideas. If we are not artists or philosophers, we may be servants of goodness, and the Good is as genuinely and surely creative as Truth and Beauty. Indeed, creative goodness pertains to each of us as an individual, as a child of God. Life is with us to carry forward our creation in His image and likeness.

The highest gift of intuition as quickened from the secret place is creative insight into the nature and powers of the individual. At times we are so fortunate as to be given this insight into another's soul. Seeing the ideal latent there we do what we can to summon it into power. We encourage, we advise, we point out opportunities. We show that the soul tends to "make circumstance," to find its creative opportunity. But better still we show that just as we have become somewhat acquainted with the secret place and begun to learn at home, so the soul we are creatively advising can learn to go to direct sources and be guided from within. Thus it may be given us to summon the soul from knowing to doing, from discipleship into leadership. The true spiritual leader has this creative touch with Life. To say this is not to claim that man as such is a creator or giver of life. There is but one Creator, one source of life. But there is a creative relation to the human spirit in the secret place. It would not be a "secret" place if we knew just why and how. Suffice it that experience itself discloses this creative presence of Life.

If you would think with the spirit, instead of merely working your brain, turn from outward things in renewed consecration to Life, lifting your problem into spiritual light to receive the heavenly guidance you may need. Give yourself time to listen, to meditate, but also give yourself time to assimilate from Life and time to grow. Remember that there is a movement from within outward, from heart to understanding. Seek, therefore, both the impetus of heart from Love and the light which shines from Wisdom. In other words, let your "leading" develop, expect it to develop in detail and become complete, just as a composer expects to develop and complete his theme till his symphony is finished. The secret place is the place of essences intuitively apprehended. What the understanding does is to work out the essence. By an "essence" one means the pure leading, the intuitively perceived whole, like the composer's theme. It may be compared to pure light. The light tends to distribute itself into even the darkest corner of the mind. Following the light and trying faithfully to live by it, we grasp the meaning of our experiences little by little, we see laws, understand principles, think from causes to effects.

With utmost confidence then one may believe in the secret place, endeavoring to live from it, to be guided by its light. All the power we once put into self-assertion we may now put into creative self-expression through this Wisdom. All the rebellion we may have felt can become harmony. All negative attitudes can give place to the positive responsiveness which makes for spiritual service. Quiet and free, open and poised at the centre, we may think and will, feel and act from the enlightened centre, with Life imbuing our life. Open at the centre, we may grow into greater responsiveness through our daily conduct, not only overcoming the nervous wear and tear, the tensions and strains which impede, but also the external activities not yet in correspondence. The ideal throughout is harmony between inner and outer, correspondence between the eternal life and the ideal in the secret place. "He that dwelleth in the secret place of the Most High shall abide under the shadow of the Almighty." "Be still, and know that I am God."

XX

HOW TO DEMONSTRATE

To demonstrate is to establish in outward expression. It is to prove, verify, know for ourselves. Its basis is either a principle which we understand and wish to exemplify, or an item of faith which we simply take on trust and hope to understand when we have proved it. Demonstration is commonly regarded as the test every individual must meet. For we have ceased to believe in teachings which bear no consequences in actual life, and it is the test which the individual makes that shows whether a belief is workable. To verify for ourselves we must come down to the concrete and observe the results in daily experience. Moreover, "the laborer is worthy of his hire," each man ought to show by the rewards or consequences which follow that his work is in accord with the spiritual law. Since there is a boundless source upon which to draw, we show our relation to it when the results prove the law of abundance.

The reason some people fail to demonstrate is

not then hard to find. They fail because their theories are too abstract, too remote from life; because they do not understand practical life well enough to know where to begin with a need immediately at hand.

The idea prevails, for example, that by holding in mind the right thought it is possible for anyone to "attract" all the conditions he desires. The thought or formula repeatedly affirmed is supposed to act like a magic influence to draw what is desired. In this way we can not only gain health without working in any other way to secure it, but win prosperity merely because we want it. Prosperity, in fact, becomes a direct object of pursuit, like a hobby. To "affirm abundance" is forthwith to gain it. One may, it is said, direct affirmative thoughts to people of wealth and draw money or other possessions from them, one may picture desired possessions and study mental influences tending to enlist the help of people who can open the way to secure these possessions. In short, to demonstrate is to procure what you want through suggestion. The principle of "mental attraction" discloses the royal road to success. The ability to "demonstrate supply" is the test of one's real power. Prosperity is a sign of salvation.

From a spiritual point of view this is contrary to order. If the laborer is "worthy of his hire," the way to prove worthy is first to do some work which merits reward according to value rendered. Therefore, first serve, first live by the spiritual law, labor for and love the more truly your fellow men. If you have greater needs and require additional resources, more co-workers, more money: then give more freely, express yourself more fully, make manifest your faith through actual service. If certain kinds of spiritual work bring greater results and you are prompted to enlarge your sphere of usefulness, consecrate yourself anew to these opportunities. Begin at the centre, not on the circumference. Do not follow the inverted order by first seeking "things" that "the kingdom" may be added, but seek first the kingdom of God and find a place to serve in a work which is making for the fuller realization of that kingdom here on earth. It is not a question of personal influence at all, since one has no desire to "attract" things from people by any insidious process. It is not primarily a question of affirmation, since affirmation must be followed by work entitling one to its rewards. Nor is it essentially a matter of attraction, as if one's inner fitness had nothing to do with circumstances. There is indeed correspondence between inward need and outward supply, but this attraction is by spiritual law, not by caprice. The prime consideration is service which prepares the way for more favorable conditions as rapidly as the soul becomes worthy. It is Divine law which presides over the selection of conditions, not our own desire.

If we begin by affirming all perfection as present with us now, denying that man ever learns or gains anything by experience, ignoring nature and making light of natural law, we put ourselves into an artificial world of thought remote from life as whole-hearted people know it. Affirming perfection in the abstract, claiming for ourselves what is true of God only, we then wonder why health, freedom and prosperity do not come our way. It is very difficult for anybody, however wise, to teach us anything while we remain in this theoretical position; for we have cut ourselves off from all sources of knowledge. Where all is claimed as accomplished and perfect now, there is of course nothing to be desired, nothing to do; hence nothing comes to us with life in it.

A return to natural conditions is devoutly to be desired for all who have isolated themselves from growth through experience. There may be other and more direct means of quickening us than through the slowly moving processes of our understanding. But not even intuition or "revelation" gives us sure knowledge "out of hand." Any principle offered us as truth becomes true for us only when we have proved it by experience. That is precisely what we mean by "demonstration." We do not really know until we have lived. Actual life is likely to be different from our expectations. We need the open mind. It is detrimental to be tied to a theory which is like an anchor to windward.

Since there is order or sequence in all things, no one can really make a leap beyond the conditions which the soul needs, whatever illusions to the contrary there may be. Since there is correspondence between inner and outer conditions, what the soul really attracts is what is needed. The law of change is from within outward, not to conditions created in imagination by ignoring natural law and the spiritual ideal, but to circumstances essential to inner development. We cannot "demonstrate over" nature, although we may seem to, for example, when we steadily reduce the amount of food, rest and sleep we take with the assumption that these matters depend solely on our thought about them. We cannot change one hair white or black in the actual world to be faced and understood. Our road lies through the conditions which people ignore when they indulge in abstract affirmations. There is no such thing as evasion in the moral realm. Action and reaction are still equal. No alleged royal road can compare with the one which is disclosed when we frankly acknowledge actual motives and seek God's help for real needs.

True demonstration is never the result of self-assertion. It is only in part a consequence of consciously chosen ends. More truly, it is a co-operative result, involving experiences we did not foresee and a wisdom greater than our own. It comes from inner adjustment and willingness to let Life have its way through us. Any prayer we may utter in our effort to attain it should include the Christian qualification, "Thy will, not mine, be done."

Our actual spiritual state is a condition, not a theory. We need not fear to look at things as they seem to be. True courage is not afraid of illusions, shadows or errors. We may look with open eye straight through any "claim" that besets us, noting its sources and associations, its hold upon us, and the point of contact which made our servitude possible. It is truth that sets men free, not the assertion of freedom when we dare not look at our own past lest we enter into it again. We are never really free until we understand, and when the vision comes the clouds clear away by themselves. We are then in the position of the one who, mistaking a stump for a bear in the dark forest, has marched up to the harmless thing and found out that it is merely a stump. What we need is the right interpretation of things as they are.

On the other hand, it is as easy to fail to demonstrate by being too much absorbed in mere conditions and processes. If some overdo the matter in one direction by ignoring the conditions of spiritual development, others go to the extreme in the opposite direction by analyzing too much and becoming enveloped in details. The newer methods of healing are, on the whole, a reaction against the old-time introspection with its emphasis on our sins and the need for acknowledging our errors and mistakes. The reaction is a sound one and has come to stay. What we now need is primary emphasis on the Spirit which accomplishes, with willingness to learn the essential lessons of life while not dwelling too long on mere details.

To demonstrate is to disconnect our attention from mere processes and unite in consciousness with the higher level of life, give our thought to the Spirit. To demonstrate is to turn about and become affirmative in every respect in which our attitude is still negative. When we are determinately positive we may learn the lessons of past experience without entering into details and conditions. There are times for looking back to learn and times when we should cut free as if the past had never existed.

To demonstrate one should not attempt to overcome everything at once. Sufficient unto the day is the problem we can best begin to solve today. When we give our attention to that, concentrating our efforts upon the immediate practical need, we find that demonstration means, *grounding things ideal in things actual.* To demonstrate is to be specific, concrete, definite. Hence we make progress toward the perfect demonstration when we limit our interests and our thoughts, with one central purpose before us, with the eye single to truth. Thus a man begins to demonstrate in earnest when he dares to stand for what he believes is true in an actual instance relating him with his fellow men today, although what he believes may not be popular and what he does may require great courage.

Frequently, our efforts fall short because we indulge in so many aspirations in various directions that we make headway in none. Here is a man, for example, who is high-strung, nervous, intense and emotional in great degree. He never permits anyone to pass him, he rushes when he works, eats with nervous haste, and writes with restless rapidity. His good resolutions lead to nothing. He affirms his general "oneness with God" to little effect. He receives treatment from an abstractionist healer, but nothing comes of it. At last he takes himself in the act, resolves to master one habit at a time, and begins by practising upon his handwriting, making each stroke of the pen with moderation, concentrating his attention upon the actual movements of his hand. The result is a pleasure he has never before experienced in his life, a sense of power in doing something with inner control. He sees at last what poise is, not as an assumed state, but one that a person can grow into throughout one's life, a state that is gradually developed through performing activities with inner control and concentration. He now makes steady headway because he is taking over a habit which hitherto simply swept him forward to do its restless bidding. So any of us might make headway if we would resolutely face something to be conquered by meeting it with a consciousness of what it is in us that wins all victories.

To adapt oneself to Life's way instead of trying to find a short cut of our own, is to realize anew that all real efficiency is from God. Both the driving force (love) and the directing force (wisdom) are from Him. What we ought to demonstrate is the Divine image and likeness, not the psychological presentment which gratifies our vanity. We wish, if our desires have really become spiritual, to find God's way and walk in it wherever it may lead, whether the vicissitudes of the path are what we prefer or not. We do not know ourselves in entirety yet. We are not aware of all the conditions to be met or all the elements to be overcome. We should not then claim to know the appropriate times and seasons. As human beings we are not managers of the conditions which best develop the soul. We are not here to dictate terms. At best we trust our guide may find us ready, when Wisdom speaks, when Love impels. What must be "demonstrated over" is our selfishness or self-love, and the victory over self is won only through heavenly aid.

Hence the power of the Spirit is the only real power that demonstrates. If our spirit bears witness together with the Holy Spirit that these heavenly things are true, so that we will to follow in the Spirit's way, then what comes by way of proof is sign and symbol of what has been divinely wrought in us. The "signs following," the first-fruits which show what went before, are needed to teach us the law of perfect demonstration; because only when spiritual realities have been ultimated or expressed do they become complete. The power which seemed to be in the human will alone, or in the Spirit welcomed in reverential receptivity, was in neither exclusively. The human spirit had to be willing. God had to be at hand. But the Spirit's might is seen when God and man in union conquer outward circumstances through inward victory. The full truth is never seen till the thing is done. The abundant life is the life of full practical realization in the flesh, in natural things. "By their fruits ye shall know them."

If I am still minded to ask, How then shall I demonstrate? the answer is not that I must wait until God does His part. Mere watchful waiting may be as far from the right attitude as the old-time attitude of Christian resignation. The spiritual law is that I should act from God's power "as if" that power were my own. Unless I make the effort, unless I put forth the energy to conquer something that is before me, such as a tendency to drive forward with restless energy, I do not put myself in line with the Life that is here to win the victory. My part is to show that I am ready to take the practical initiative, and follow up my prayers with deeds done.

Let us make the matter simple. Here is a day when one feels an inward need. There is a difficulty to be overcome, a problem to be solved, or someone to be helped. Let me then go apart by myself and seek the quiet sanctuary of the Spirit once more. "Be still, and know that I am God," I say to myself, with the realization that God is present like an Over-soul to guide and illumine me. May I trust in Him so that my mind shall be "stayed" upon His wisdom. May I be at peace so that some measure of His peace shall touch my spirit with tranquillity. Then may I see the way in the special direction in which I need light.

What I affirm as true, now, is the God-ward part of my life, the perfect peace in which the Father can keep me, the infinite wisdom adequate to meet all occasions, the perfect love which casts out all fear. If I did not lack this peace there would be no reason for seeking it. If I realized all wisdom I should have no problem to bring forward for solution. If perfect love controlled my heart I should not have "one fear to conquer each day." Inevitably then I must take an attitude in my quest for help which admits a lack, with humility or readiness enough to make me receptive. Since the Father already knows the way whereon I should walk, since He has provided for every need, my part is to listen and make myself ready in the secret place that I may receive what the Father has provided.

What I must do, therefore, in order to demonstrate is to put out of the way whatever thought, attitude of will, emotion, habit, deed or mode of conduct there may be that interferes with the coming of what the Father has provided. Then when my thinking, my willing and my conduct follow the spiritual order, I may indeed make use of my imaging power, my affirmations and all the rest of my psychological equipment, to foster the things of the Spirit. The hard part for most of us is to attain the spiritual order. We want things to come in our way and when we want them. We would like to sail serenely down the stream of time with everything that could gratify human desire floating to us out of the air, while we smilingly discourse on the success of our demonstrations. But that is not the order of things in the spiritual life. Interiorly we have only what we deserve. What we now possess came to us in relation to what we were. We tried "to get" rather than to give. We worked hard to accumulate possessions and now we propose to enjoy them. We looked out for Number One. At first thought these new teachings about suggestion and the subconscious mind seem to afford a still more successful way of putting self first. But sober second thought shows that in all things there reigns a spiritual law such that we need to seek the Spirit first, we need to give, to be, to make manifest. When we have made the great effort, that is, in the overcoming of self and self-love, we shall find that matters are righting themselves and seeking new positions in relation to the new inner centre of equilibrium.

The new teaching of our time shows how to begin more immediately where beginnings are effective, that is, with ourselves. No one who sincerely wishes to live by the spiritual law will find himself without guidance. There is always something at hand to begin upon. There is always some word of wisdom we can begin to apply. To demonstrate is to begin. To begin is to find the little becoming more. "God helps those who help themselves." And this deeper self-helpfulness means in the language of the new philosophy of healing a growing recognition on our part of "the Science of the Christ."

To be prepared to demonstrate in the most successful way, therefore, we need to be as well equipped as we can in knowledge of what we have defined in the foregoing chapters as "the priceless possession." There should no longer be any theoretical barrier which keeps us from looking directly to the supreme sources of life and wisdom. There is in very truth a spiritual science which we may all begin to apply, to verify for ourselves. There is for all an ideal of Christian living which is workable here and now. This science we may adopt and practise as a science which is true in its own right over and above or apart from any particular interpretation of the Gospels that may be espoused by a given sect. Hence it is well to carry the inquiry into this science far enough to have a practical way of thinking about the human Jesus and the resurrection or glorification, always keeping in mind that from the point of view of spiritual health and healing these are practical, not theological, matters.

That is to say, nearly everyone who owns allegiance to a sect or denomination of the Christian Church is likely to take exception to the distinction drawn between "the Christ" as considered above, Chap. III, and "the human Jesus," *when it is a question of theology.* Some will prefer the teaching of the Episcopal Church, hence will emphasize the Pauline Epistles, and will speak of "our Lord." Others will reinterpret what follows so that the human Jesus will become "the Lord." Still others will prefer the title of "the Son of God." We plead for the direct reading of the Gospels themselves as guides to practical life and spiritual healing, since this distinction between Jesus and the Christ has proved so helpful. Each reader will then be free in other connections to reinterpret as he chooses. For the present we are concerned with the gospel of healing. The acknowledgment of the Lord should bring this practical realization. To demonstrate in Christian terms is thus to carry our idealism concerning the Christ into the ultimate. To demonstrate is to see that regeneration of some sort should follow. Hence we need to carry our practical thought through to the end.

XXI

SUMMARY AND DEFINITION

I

THE term "spiritual healing" as we have been using it in these pages indicates both the source of power and the special method employed. The efficiency is attributed, not to human thought, not to the individual will, self, or attitude; but to the Divine presence realized through inner responsiveness and co-operation, and made forceful through the human spirit as means or agency. The special method involves the attitude and agencies of the inner life, through the use of silent meditation, control of the energies centring about the self, poise, peace, and an affirmative faith made practical through psychological knowledge. This method is further distinguished by the effort of those who employ it to understand and overcome the more serious difficulties of the life of suffering, to gain freedom for the individual, and to solve the more central problems of those who are sensitively organized. Spiritual healing has for its object the actual overcoming of the inner causes and conditions which produce ill-health and misery, in contrast with methods which deal with surfaces only. Thus it involves not merely temporary alleviation of human ills, and the help which one soul can give another; but an educational process extending out into the social world. It may begin and usually does start with the alleviation of pain, and the use of "silent treatment" for those who are unable as yet to draw upon inner resources for themselves. It may at first be wholly concerned with problems of ill-health. But presently it leads to character-building, the "soul's problem" or the mastery of temperament, and the whole question of "salvation" or the new birth. It changes from the silent method to conversational studies, the art of the spiritual life, and spiritual re-education.

Spiritual healing, therefore, like the original Christianity, ministers to the whole individual, as a physical or natural being, as mental and social, moral and spiritual. Thus it takes all the facts and conditions of disease and suffering into account, ignoring nothing. It frankly faces the facts of heredity and environment, the given social atmosphere, noting man's multiform nature, conscious and subconscious. But whatever the character and force of the external circumstances in a given case, the centre of activity is found in the inner life. Hence the method employed implies the use of those superior agencies accessible to the human spirit which touch the heart. If, for example, "perfect love casteth out fear," we are concerned not with the fears to be cast out but with the conditions that enlist the aid of "perfect love." If there is an inner peace which "passeth all understanding," we must endeavor to rise above our ordinary mental processes to realize this peace through actual inner experience.

The surpassing gift which our age has bestowed upon us is this immediate spiritual clue to the resources of the Divine presence. Too often in the past God has been merely historical, heaven elsewhere, and spiritual realities mere matters to read about. It has seemed to many that if they could not conform to the established usages and beliefs of the Church their faith would go. The new age assures us that Divine realities are not dependent on time or place, on creeds, institutions or books; but on the individual's recognition and use. Here, in the priceless eternity which is ever ours, there resides all the power, the wisdom, the love and peace we need. We need not make the effort difficult. We need not look for the marvellous. Wherever placed and however constituted, we may begin today to look within and above, basing our faith on the conviction that man is by nature so fashioned as to live in the spiritual world, to apprehend the

Divine presence and to live by it. We may in a measure need to look back to great historical scenes in the spiritual life to regain the impetus, but only that we may recover the Christianity which ministers to the whole man.

To be sure, one must in a measure become aware of the urgent needs in oneself and others. We all have our repressed emotional states, our dissatisfactions and interior conflicts. We lack repose, we give way to fancies, worries, excitements. Few of us possess sufficient control and mental co-ordination to use all our energies to advantage. It is difficult for most of us to draw a line of distinction between the fleshly organism and the soul, hence much effort is required to work our way into the inner life as a conscious centre of reality open to Divine resources. Yet we need not urge ourselves. The first step is to become inwardly still, that we may by contrast realize the difference between the outward play of consciousness and the inward activity which, through its intervals, makes known the finer energies of the spirit.

Disease is inefficiency, scattering of force, nervous constraint, tension. This is seen in the case of one who is over-zealous in the effort to get ahead in the world, who is self-coercive, insistent, drawing upon the supply of nerve-energy to the limit, and suffering from the subsequent exhaustion and collapse. It is seen in the case of one who is morbidly self-conscious, unsocial, cut off from the usual activities of domestic life, hence repressed, cramped in spirit. There is much more to be said about ill-health than this. The general physician would add his physiological diagnosis, the nerve-specialist his description, and so on. But we are here concerned with crucial matters. At heart the over-zealousness which expresses itself in nervous tensions and exhaustion may spring from undue love of self and the world, from a certain ambition or ruling desire which must be understood and corrected. The true cure comes with the discovery that what we truly desire, what we can best do in the world, is possible through quiet self-knowledge and interior control, through thoughtful adjustment to life. Health in this sense is spiritual efficiency, the wise use of all our forces from the centre; it is spiritual freedom and adequate self-expression through the Divine purpose.

We are all at some stage of the journey on this the highway of life. We were started forth by incentives which we did not understand. We have had experiences which we never consciously sought. But what truly impelled us one and all was longing for the fulness of life, desire to find our place and do our work in the world. We have not proceeded at random, although this has often seemed to be the case. We have passed through the testing-times that we needed. Each man of us belongs where he is today. There is no reason to complain, spiritually speaking. What is called for is, awareness of the situation, the fact of correspondence between inner circumstance and type, between our real environment and the purpose to be realized through co-operation with Divine guidance.

When we gain the inner point of view we realize that life is constituted for the welfare of the soul, with all the laws, powers, guidances and conditions required. Being thus organized, life could not at the same time be for external things simply. Life is adapted to that which is most worth while, to freedom, truth, beauty, service; heaven, order, harmony, mutual life as "members one of another," howbeit man has tried to take life as if meant for the realization of his desire *to possess outward things* to the exclusion of his brother and the neglect of God. Naturally we are perplexed and mystified, till we learn this. As naturally we mistake the physical organism for the soul, searching for external causes of our disquietude and misery, disparaging life and condemning our Maker. Inevitably our friction increases, while in our ignorance and self-will we persist in going counter to Life.

Spiritual healing reverses all this. It shows

us that we are in process, frequently suffering from a sense of division within the self. By contrast we then learn that we have mistaken the process for the efficiency, the means for the end; we have even mistaken this wonderful instrument of ours, the physical organism, for the individual who uses it. Thus we have become imprisoned within the flesh, swept off our feet by whirlwinds of excitement and fear, our substance gnawed by nervous friction. Thus we have moved on from moment to moment in the mere feeling or thought of the passing hour; living in fragments, shifting from mood to mood. We have had no sense of unity or wholeness, no interior consistency or constancy. Sometimes we have striven, sometimes we have yielded. Now we have prayed, and now rebelled as if the whole world were against us. Some of us have been far too self-assertive, while others have surrendered too frequently. Thus we have lacked balance, repose.

What is the faith that makes whole? What was meant when the Master said, "Thy faith hath made thee whole?" Surely, the Divine love thus appealing to the soul through the open channel of faith touched the entire individual, not with reference to sin or disease alone. Such was the openness, the responsiveness of spirit on the part of those who came for salvation (wholeness), that the entire inner life was ready, gave itself in aspiration. That which we intellectual mortals strive to attain by varied efforts during the weeks and months and years was thereby achieved all at once. All the inner obstacles gave way, the fears vanished, the excitements subsided, the worries ceased, the tensions were removed, the suppressions yielded. The real inner self was thereby called into play. Such healing was in fact *creative,* it produced a new combination of powers, achieved a synthesis amidst hitherto conflicting forces. Would that you and I could so fully give ourselves to the Spirit! Would that whole groups could so give themselves that the Holy Spirit should, as of old, fall upon all who hear, overcoming all separateness!

The ideal of all spiritual healing is unison with God regarded as creative love and guiding wisdom. Through this conjunction one realizes that this end is what the Divine power has all the time been working for although we did not know it. This conjunction is not attained through mere humility or self-effacement; for the human soul is not a mere medium or "receptacle," and we cannot remain in the period of childhood. The soul is primarily *active,* whatever the attitude. We are by no means merely receptive, for example, when we complain, when we fear, rebel, lose patience, become wrought up, nervous, excited. Nor are we quiescent when we are pessimistic, self-centred, selfish. All these are active states, and when we generate misery for ourselves we are affirmative, though in a mistaken way. What we need to do is, "about face" and use the same energy in accord with Life, not against it. All the power we employ when we are spiteful, angry, jealous, mean, distrustfül; when we agonize and become self-coercive, or try to control others, is in itself good; it is primarily a question of the right use of our energies.

The Divine life in its instreaming is, as we have seen, unmistakably dynamic, the wisdom is for our active use, and the love for our quickening. Unless we use the life that comes to us we can hardly expect more. This means that the peace our spirits feel is not for our private devotions alone, not for mere piety but to be manifested socially, in the voice, in the countenance, in service. It means that unless we change our attitude from self-love and the love of things to love of God and our fellow men we will not continue to receive. It means that unless we think for ourselves we do not appropriate the Divine wisdom.

Here is where the practical method of realizing the presence of God comes to our aid. Instead of merely enjoying, acquiescing, as many do when they listen to sermons and other parts of a service in church, thereby losing the impetus which calls for prompt response, we endeavor actively to enter into and make our own the life which is for our health, freedom, and social expression. We are aware that we must feel or experience first in order to know; then we must think vividly, assimilate, appropriate. Moreover, we well know that we must live first before we can help others. But the goal of realization is service through the power of example, through composure, inner freedom, control, poise. Every element of the inner process of realization is a means to an end. It is the social self that is called into wholeness of expression. The faith that makes whole appeals to the entire individual, to stand forth, to be thankful, glad, free, sane.

II

The ability to realize the Divine presence for purposes of healing implies the possession by the soul or spirit of higher powers than those that are conditioned by the body, that is, intuition, spiritual receptivity, spiritual sight: spiritual senses acting independently of the physical senses. Thus one is able to communicate with and heal people at a distance, and healers possessing intuition in marked degree can discern the states of their patients during "absent healing." The ability to disconnect the attention from the lower level of consciousness and concentrate it upon the higher level, in quest of Divine guidance, is also spiritual.

We start then with the fact that by turning aside from the ordinary rush of consciousness on the natural level one may connect one's active centre with a finer stream of energies and so apply those energies as to produce changes in consciousness, in mental attitude, and so (by making an impression that counts) inducing subconscious after-effects and bodily results. The emphasis is on the dynamic presence of God, and on the affirmative response of the soul. One thinks of the spiritual mind (the inner centre, secret place, "mind of Christ") as immediately open to the Divine life, according to need, and of the spontaneous flow of thought as the first result of this quickening. Thought in this sense (thought with the spirit, in spiritual light) is affirmative in high degree, directive, a vehicle of the Creative Presence. It uses mental imagery, ideas, directions of mind favoring ideals, forceful attention or concentration, *at will.* The spiritual activity is the central consideration. The mental picturing or creation of ideals, the realizational process or the particular thought employed, the affirmation selected, is instrumental. The subconscious result follows upon the vivid mental impression, the dynamic moment. The essential is to find the inner kingdom, find God. The changed centre of spiritual equilibrium then brings its quickening consequences. The specific thoughts that occupy the mind, during the fifteen minutes or so which constitute the silent treatment, develop out of the centralizing activity. That is to say, the *activity* is more fundamental, more widely inclusive than any one phase of the process, such as affirming, realizing, concentrating on mental pictures, focussing the attention.

The physicist would argue that this breaks the law of conservation of energy. But he limits energy to the natural world, and shuts mental life into a region apart. We do not sunder the natural from the mental in this manner, but look to the spiritual realm as the basis of causality, the one ultimate source of energy. Consequently, there is no chasm to bridge, no loss or creation of energy when a spiritual impulse goes forth to produce changes in the body through the brain. It is primarily a question of transmutation or sublimation, a different direction given to the same energy. To say this is to hold that the soul is essentially a centre of activity—not of mere thought.

The soul may seem to be determined by bodily processes, and so indeed it is for most of us, most of the time. Thus we mistake processes for the activity that stirs within them. Thus we become prisoners of nerves, of the brain, of habits, moods, directions of mind, stereotyped modes of thought, customary modes of feeling, and the like. But it need not be so. We can learn to reverse the process, living and thinking with the activity that produces, giving allegiance to the Life within this activity. Thus the external mental processes may be determined by the interior spiritual states, and the brain may be controlled by first controlling the spirit.

To give assent to a wave of angry excitement or passion is to permit the soul to become a storm centre. To turn away from the violent emotion and connect with the stream of peace-energy is to feel a different mode of motion and to give forth a different kind of vibration. Here is the process in barest outline. You may call it either transmutation of energy, transfer of attention or upliftment of spiritual consciousness, as you will. The essential is to gain this power in some measure, then to increase it. When you win it you will have a basis in actual experience on which to build.

As here regarded, the soul is in ideal a unity, however many the phases of consciousness. On the lower level, the soul is brought into relation with the activities of the body, through the volitions which we cannot consciously observe because they occur so quickly. For example, when one jumps out of a chair, one is merely aware of a quickly formed decision to which the organism responds by habit. A little higher, the activity is more conscious and intellectual. There is less accompanying physical activity. The world of motion is represented by means of ideas. Higher still, the soul is active in modes that conceivably will survive after death. This is the level of clairvoyance, clairaudience, the perception of mental atmospheres, communication with persons at a distance "psychically." The soul is both active and passive on this level (passivity is minimum activity). That is, one may become consciously receptive, in the effort to catch a thought from another at a distance, to discern a person's interior state according to Quimby's intuitive method; one may be spontaneously receptive, as in the case of an interior illumination which the mind merely watches for the time; or one may send one's activities forth in direct co-operation with the Spirit. By contrast one is aware through experience of the difference between this higher level and the ordinary round of experiences.

What one feels is a finer vibration, a great peace, a sense of inward repose. The inner self thus touched, the personality as a whole responds. The higher activity once received, it may be directed according to need, or sent forth to another. To seek this inner communion day by day is to grow in repose, refinement, equanimity. The active centre thus developed is a vantage-point in times of stress, a centre of reserve-power whither one may turn in perfect confidence, well knowing that there is a boundless supply behind, that the activities of the lower level cannot prevail against it.

Only with faltering words can one suggest the experience at its best. Beyond the point where analysis penetrates there is a Presence whose power lifts the soul to unwonted heights. There one has a vision of the unity of life, the Divine order, the wise beauty. Things and events fit together, their meaning is seen. One thinks not so much of the present moment or the next deed, as of the fulness of life's perfect round. Here one beholds the reality itself about which in other moments one merely philosophizes. One lives with the world-system. One abides with God in the eternal. One is not so much concerned with growth as with the world of the formative Spirit. One seems almost to hear the word before it is made flesh, one helps to make it flesh by accepting the spiritual law. One beholds all events from the point of view of the ideal, the details of their development seem of minor importance. Yet one receives a new impetus to action, a new desire to share these heavenly gifts with all whose vision is less clear. The resulting practical impetus is the best evidence one can give of the sanity and value of these experiences.

How shall one begin? Simply by starting with what is clear and letting the rest follow. Here you are, a human soul. Here is human life, loving, tender, sympathetic. Here is God, the All-Father: you believe in His presence, His guiding love and wisdom. Cling to this relationship, and lift the soul in responsiveness. You are alive and have problems. Others are alive and have their problems. In association with you are those who share your aspirations, whose contact with you enlists your better selfhood. Study these associations to learn what you are by what you do, to learn where you stand in the spiritual process. Discover what is even now taking place, how the present is leading to the future, what you are becoming.

God is here in the common. Do not strain after Him. See Life in what you are passing through today, and let Life have its course. Be calm at the centre, that you may truly respond. Remember that the spiritual world is the more real world, is around us here and now. There is no space between, no time intervening. You are a spirit now, even in this apparently insignificant life-round. Do not postpone the highest and best.

But remember this. The soul sees quickly and far in the superior realm, assimilates power and wisdom without regard to time. Thereupon the more slowly working intellectual process begins a corresponding assimilation. The flesh responds more slowly than the understanding. Therefore, when you have dwelt on the heights for a season, give mind and body time to respond. Do not push them. Do not think that you have fallen back or lost hold, even though the way is dark and you cannot see beyond physical sensation. Give yourself time to grow. Let yourself grow in Life's way. Keep your eye upon the heights, but be moderate and faithful when clouds veil the summit.

If you would help another, let love lead the way. The desire to help is a prayer for the power of spiritual healing. The silent, deeply poised attitude is dynamic. Hold to this and adopt supplementary methods only so far as may be needed. There is guidance at hand for each step of the way. There is a "stream of tendency" or power. Pause and observe that you may learn whither the stream is flowing. Do not judge by the sensations. Live wholly in consciousness of the readjustments which Life is carrying forward. Trust Life and let your dynamic attitude be quickened by it, in guided co-operation.

III

Quimby's intuitive method differed from the affirmative method now employed by those who use suggestion as the chief agency in healing. The first dependence was put upon intuitive impressions gained by sitting silently by the sick, and rendering the mind (the spiritual senses) inwardly open to discern the inner conditions and causes. The process included (1) discernment of the real interior inner mental state or attitude, for example, rebellion, complaint, fear, nervous excitement, bitterness; (2) knowledge of the opinion or belief concerning the ailment, the name attached to it, the physician's diagnosis or the patient's misinterpretation; and (3) insight into the actual condition of the organism in contrast with the fancied condition or the patient's belief. Thus suppressed grief might be a cause, worry over the notion that one had committed the unpardonable sin, domestic unhappiness, worry over financial and other affairs; while the supposed cause might be some physical symptom of slight moment. The actual cause discerned, one could proceed to "the wisdom of the situation," the truth which would set the patient free. The "silent treatment" took its two-fold clue in this way: from the need of the patient and from the Divine truth, and varied with the case, the need, the special occasion. The process was realization. The healer's thought was instrumental to the therapeutic power of the Spirit. The emphasis was on the spiritual truth of the patient's being.

Since the early days, the tendency has been to substitute specific affirmations for each case, and to deny the reality of any besetting conditions. This change came about partly because in the diffusion of the silent method among many types of healers there were few who had either the intuition or the healing power of the pioneers. Then, too, some people took the work up whose interests might briefly be described as mental rather than spiritual. But if we are interested to attain the spiritual level we will naturally advance from merely mental methods as soon as we can, opening the spirit that it may grow in intuition. The affirmations or suggestions do not always "take." There are more difficult cases which do not work out in that way. There is often need of deep discernment into causes. If we find a patient in an attitude of weak or rebellious adjustment, exciting, pessimistic, self-assertive, over-sensitive, it may be necessary to persuade him through conversation to adopt a different philosophy of life. The more intimately we discern the heart the more directly we can proceed. The prime interest is: intelligently to aid the patient to understand himself spiritually, hence to begin to modify his attitude. The explanation given includes an account of the real origin of the trouble, and an ideal to follow. The appeal is to reason as well as to the spirit. The further one carries the intuitive method the more clearly one sees that no two individuals are alike, no two experiences in the silence are alike: one is led by the spirit of the occasion. At the same time one is free to make the best possible use of specific affirmations or realizations, according to the case.

One should start always with the thought of God, make vivid the idea of the Divine presence by selecting some sentence from the Bible, such as, "Be still, and know that I am God," which aids the process of detaching one's consciousness from the outer world and renews the realizational activity. Some prefer always to begin with the same sentence, since it has hallowed associations and readily admits one into the heart of the realization. Think of the Presence in the sense of vivifying power or energy, as quickening, life-giving. Consider what that Presence must be in itself, undisturbed at heart, in perfect peace, in ineffable composure, all-comprehending wisdom, all-sustaining love. Make such affirmations as best bring this realization before you.

Then see the Spirit as going forth from its

centre (which is everywhere, its circumference nowhere) in power-conveying activity or vibration, going forth into action to touch the hearts or spirits of men, imbuing them with love, guiding their minds with wisdom.

Having dwelt on the God-ward side for a time, turn to the human and see the spirit or soul in its integrity in the presence of this divinely perfect peace and composure, able to receive love and wisdom according to need.

Then put the two together: "Thou wilt keep him in perfect peace whose mind is stayed on Thee, because he trusteth in Thee." "In Him we live, and move, and have our being" in the sense that we participate in this vivifying, power-bringing Presence. The inward stillness or realization invites the presence. We speak as it were to ourselves as if for God when we say, "Be still and know that I am God." We catch for the moment the Divine point of view, seeing our own restlessness and lack of faith. We project our consciousness as if looking down from a heavenly height and stilling the tempest, bidding everything in our nature fall into line. Then it dawns upon us with clarifying consciousness that unless we always dwelt in the ineffable Presence, unless we always lived, moved, and had our being in God *in reality* (whatever the appearance), we never could exist for a moment, we never would continue to be. Our first step in realization, therefore, simply brings into consciousness that which all the way along is *the supreme truth of life.*

Having renewed our consciousness of the Divine presence in general, the next consideration is in favor of the special point on which we need help, on which another needs light. To separate one's thought as affirmatively as possible from the old associates, the old imagery, fears, thoughts, emotions, memories connected with the experience which one is endeavoring to overcome, and to make this separation clear-cut and distinctive, is to give our realization the force of a denial of the power of the old conditions in which one has been immersed. This in brief is what the victorious attitude accomplishes. It asserts so positively that one must find God that it makes light of the greatest obstacle. For this attitude means that one has so given the spirit to the ideal that one knows no such word as fail. What we have learned thus clearly for ourselves we can see clearly for another. We may take the other into the Presence, seeing him in the light of the perfect ideal, in peace, in health, in freedom. We may draw the sharpest possible line between the spirit as thus free and the old conditions. Sometimes this can best be done by realizing such freedom in general. Again, one finds it desirable to be more specific, directive. The thoughts that come and go and constitute the subject-matter of the realization, take their clue from this directive activity.

Experience shows that a realization is made definite by being directed to the actual life we are living today, from within. Hence it is important to avoid being abstract, as if experience on the natural level of consciousness did not exist at all. Sometimes indeed there is no realization which equals the thought of the realities of the higher level, the assertion of "pure spirit" as the only reality. But if we overdo this thought we may be out of touch with the very life which we wish to spiritualize. The result might be a glossing over of actual conditions and we might seem to be meeting with splendid success, even for years. But a state glossed over, like one suppressed, will have its day. That is why we find some people falling from abstract grace and beginning anew, depending on deep breathing, out-of-door exercise, vegetarian diet, and any other physical method by which they can reestablish their balance. But putting our idealism in relation to common sense we may begin as we can hold out, steadily carrying our ideals into practice. And so we find leaders going steadily on as the years pass, never falling from grace, never experiencing a relapse or recurrence of old troubles. These have kept their eyes on the stars while also walking wisely on earth. They have dared affirm the realities of the higher level without denying the lessons of the lower. They have seen the Spirit going forth into incarnation, becoming concrete in the flesh.

To be concrete, therefore, we need to realize that the Power or Life with us to heal is immediately at hand in such a way that, opportunity being granted, it tends to enter where we need it most, to proceed from the centre outward to do its regenerative work until it touches the "ultimates" or externals. The reason some have first had to learn to breathe deeply, change their diet, or overcome nervous tensions by practising relaxation, before they could make much inner headway, is found in the fact that they were beset by all these tensions, and their mere declaration of perfection on the abstract level was not sufficient. But if we understand these matters from within we can learn to take off the tensions without trying now this method of relaxation and now that, groping along for we know not precisely what. Then, working from within outward when our ideals elevate us, our tastes change, our standards become purer, we may change outwardly in response and find that the simpler, purer modes of living belong with the inner changes and have come to stay. Then as matter of habit we will keep the system freer, more and more in harmony with the things of the Spirit. The result will be constructive or creative health. We will not then be forever considering how to overcome, how to demonstrate, but will live tha tmode of life which brings with it health as a natural consequence without thinking about it.

Workers in this field have reached their present point of success by seizing upon a few practical ideas and putting them to the test, beginning wherever they happened to be and forging ahead. We should simplify. It is not a complex process, this method of healing. The details may interest us but they are not necessary. We should not expect to have these all made clear in advance of experience. There is an element which experience itself adds when we have put into use what we possess. So if we do nothing more at first than repeat a scriptural sentence, holding to it steadily, this endeavor may open the way. There is, of course, a complete spiritual science of the whole process, with its psychological elements, its spiritual principles, with knowledge of all the laws, forces and conditions. But this is rather the intellectual or philosophical part of it. There are times for reviewing this part, that we may bring all these considerations into their unity. When it comes to actual practice, however, we need to be specific and to simplify. Thus the three words, "Peace, be still," may suffice to open the inner door for us, and there we are in the realm of pure Spirit. Then, pausing a moment, a clue may disclose itself, and we are in the realm of pure Spirit with a clue or leading.

If we could at once do what we want to, in our impulsiveness, we might wish to take ourselves out of the conflict of forces. But we are in this balance between heavenly love and self-love for a purpose: to see the consequences of both, that is, that heaven or hell begins with the one or the other; to come to judgment in the living present, noting what has brought us where we stand; that we may *freely* choose, adopt a prevailing love. Then at last when we identify ourselves with love for God and man, in preference to selfishness, the conflict can be overcome, will cease. That is the whole meaning of suffering: that we may be brought to the point where we can live without it—so far as what we produce ourselves is concerned. Then we naturally turn about and begin to carry the glad news to others which will set them free also. The Divine guidance holds us down to just this concrete situation till we learn it. This is the wonder and beauty of our practical life with God. The law of the Divine-human is the great law to learn. The same law which seems an infliction while we are "under the law," as the great apostle puts it, is the law of our emancipation when we understand.

People try to evade this law who maintain that it is only a question of "applied psychology," of claiming wealth and piling up the millions, as if the goal of life were to get rich; they tell you that the spiritual can all be left out, that we need have nothing to do with religious considerations. But granted this higher insight for which we are pleading, it becomes plain that all the psychological machinery, so to speak, may be lifted up to the higher level. Then we may see with crystal clearness that "the laborer is worthy of his hire," that there is a law of spiritual abundance such that what we need for our life and work in the world will be forthcoming so far as we are prepared, when we respond and move from within outward. The law exists to "bring us to Christ," to give us "the mind of Christ." It compels us to reap as we have sown, that we may learn its power over us. There is no such thing as demonstration over it by the human will or by human thought alone. To put prosperity first in rank is to fail to find it in the true sense at all. But prosperity *according to what we deserve* is indeed, like constructive health, one of the fruits of the Spirit, one of the things that are added, that follow. The essential is to seek the Spirit.

XXII

SPIRITUAL PSYCHOLOGY

We come now, in conclusion, to certain questions of a psychological nature which need to be considered if vistas for further thought and study are to be opened before us. These questions are often asked. They are on the whole secondary questions, and yet the pathway of advance into the spiritual life is the more thoroughly cleared if we regard them as of interest in themselves.

For example, the question is often raised whether or not it is possible to explain spiritual healing on the basis of "suggestion." Many writers on the subject believe that such healing can be thus explained. Indeed, they hold that it is merely a question of applied psychology, anyway, and so-called spiritual thought need not be introduced at all. They insist that suggestion is the prime factor, whether understood and acknowledged or not. And they seem to have scored a point in the argument against devotees of this or that spiritual faith, as if the whole idea of our relationship to God and the spiritual life were superfluous.

From the point of view of this book the theory of suggestion is adequate only so far as the mental elements of the healing process are concerned, that is, only so far as it is a question of telepathy or thought transference, and of the changes of mind wrought in the patient other than regenerative or spiritual changes.

It has long been recognized, for example, that in order for the therapeutist's suggestion to take effect in the mind of the percipient there must be predisposing conditions, such as faith or expectant attention. The percipient's favorable attitude amounts to self-suggestion. This auto-suggestion would no doubt explain many of the results occurring at sacred shrines where so-called miracles of healing take place, and in all instances where there is no activity from without sufficient to produce a decisive change within. It would then be a question of the favoring conditions in the percipient's mentality as a whole, in contrast with any element of his nature which might act as a counter-suggestion.

Mr. Myers long ago contended that "not one suggestion in a million reaches or influences the subliminal self,"—that portion of our nature which lies below the level or threshold of ordinary consciousness. But even in the case of the one suggestion which is instrumental in producing a cure, the suggestion must be something more than a name or form of words. There must follow, as Mr. Myers has shown more plainly than most writers on the subject, a profound nervous change started by some powerful nervous stimulus from without or within.[1] Granted this change following upon the suggestion, what are its conditions, what are the forces at work, and what lies back of the nervous activities? What is healing in its final analysis?

Suppose we agree that suggestion conveyed by telepathy is the instrumental cause in many cases, what shall we say about those cases where the favoring auto-suggestions and conditions are lacking, and where there are so many inhibitions or counter-suggestions in the percipient's nature that it is practically impossible to introduce a suggestion edgewise? Spiritual healers have succeeded when there was no faith, when there was pronounced opposition in mental attitude, when, in fact, all known conditions were unfavorable. They have maintained that there is a higher or more direct access to a patient's inner nature than by means of thought transference. Indeed, some have insisted that no suggestion of theirs could have produced

[1] "Human Personality and its Survival of Bodily Death."

such a decisive effect as sometimes results. It may well be that "vibration" is transferred, they will say. But at times there is less mental activity or "thought," the realization seems to be almost wholly that of maintaining an inner state, a state of peace and exceptional command in the "inner centre." The favoring process set up within the patient is incidental to a higher activity, of which the nervous change is only an expression. The decisive activity appears to be spiritual in type. To the therapeutist the "thoughts" he thinks seem to be incidental, just as his personality is secondary. He seems to be rather a partner to an experience which does indeed manifest itself in his thoughts, but which is greater in power than they are, a spiritual experience which he shares but does not assume wholly to control. And to drop out the idea of these beatific values in favor of suggestion as decisive would seem to be to lose a supreme reality.

Mr. Myers maintained that there is "some unknown cause" which determines whether the suggestion is to "take" or no. Looking further than the theory of suggestion can carry us, he finds it imperative to believe it possible by a "right disposition of our minds to draw energy from an environing world of spiritual life." The real question then is, What is it that touches the spring which moves us so potently in our deeper selfhood? How is it that we draw strength from the unseen? It is plainly something dynamic within us that is set free. But this attitude of the heart or response of the secret place of the spirit is the prime essential which we have been considering all along in the preceding pages. The majority of readers will care more to learn under what conditions it is to be attained than to explain the psychological process. And plainly there is a very great advantage in assigning the efficiency directly to the Eternal Presence, whatever the mental aids may be.

Why is it that even when the theory of spiritual healing is stated clearly and persuasively it is still difficult in some cases to put it into practice?

There are several reasons. Our conventional education proceeds on the assumption that the human mind is chiefly intellect, that we have reached the "age of reason" in the world at large, and all that is necessary is to find the right form of words, the persuasive argument. Mental healing in all its forms still shows the effect of this intellectualism, hence the emphasis on the "power of thought" and on suggestion, to the neglect of the will and the other mental elements, as I have shown at length elsewhere.[1] We cling to the notion that the intellect is something like three-fourths of life, despite Matthew Arnold's wise remark that "conduct is three-fourths of life." Therefore when our intellectual methods fail we are nonplussed.

Meanwhile, our nature as a whole is intimately related to the unconscious and the subconscious. There is, for example, the whole range of instincts, including the instinct for self-preservation, the sexual instinct, and all those promptings which manifest curiosity, imitativeness, and the like. These actuate the human being long before there is consciousness of them. So, too, our desires and emotions begin on an impulsive or unconscious basis; we are aware of feelings of pleasure and pain because of processes going on which were originally pre-conscious. Again, our habits are outgrowths of the unconscious. Consciousness in anything like an explicit sense comes in with choice, that is, with thought and will, when the self is developed enough to intervene, emphasizing some of the desires, trying to outwit others. As highly developed as thought may be, the major part of mental life still remains below the threshold, carried on subconsciously, as we say. Our whole conscious life is a progressive discovery

[1] "Handbook of the New Thought."

of the elements of our nature which have been operative all along but over which we have had little control. If our technique is to become complete it must take all these elements into account, also our suppressions and repressions, our dissatisfactions and inner conflicts, especially our inhibitions. We are not carried very far by assuming that the chief obstacles within us are "wrong thoughts." They are much more likely to be misunderstood or unexpressed desires and emotional complexes. All these may act as counter-suggestions to offset a healer's work. Hence the necessity of carrying that work much further than suggestions can carry it, in favor of deeply interior spiritual understanding.

Now, mental healing may indeed be lifted to the spiritual level by realizations involving the idea of "the Christ within," and the results may greatly surpass explanation. That is to say, the healer may have touched some of these submerged elements of a patient's nature without knowing what he was touching. For there is ordinarily no such penetrating insight into the deeper self as made possible the remarkable pioneer work of P. P. Quimby in this field. But what is needed is an adequate spiritual psychology, a science of all these mental and spiritual elements centering about the will or "prevailing love" with its accompanying activities.

These deeper activities include, for instance, the so-called "besetting sin," the temperamental problem. Spiritual therapy sometimes falls short by aiming at mere harmony, inner poise or control, without touching upon the more central question of self-love, self-esteem or selfishness. It does not always push through to the point of radical changes in conduct, in "the life." But in many instances it is plain that there is need of something more searching than "transmutation" or "sublimation." The newly formed habit of enjoying "the silence" is not enough. Nor are all matters cleared up by reading or by attending lectures and taking lessons. The pathway that is "straight and narrow" still lies ahead for some of the devotees. Individual salvation is no more adequate in the realm of health than it is in the Church, since the real consideration after all is regeneration, is change into the life of service. The true "Christ within" is social, universal, and this Christ is not attained by complacently identifying oneself with the Christ in interior contemplation.

In short, there appears to be no suggestion, silence, sublimation of lower emotions or transmutation of unworthy desires, which takes the place of the Christian necessity of coming to judgment and seeing things *as they are;* and sometimes a person's illnesses and troubles are so connected with this the deepest problem of the soul that there is no freedom except through regeneration. In a way this is true of all of us. The method of spiritual healing is another way of finding it out. We realize after a time that the initiatives do not all rest with the individual, as if everything within us could be controlled by thought. We need all the development possible in this direction. We need a complete technique for disclosing the subconscious. But there is also need of the consecration to spiritual service which in the case of Quimby and his more ardent followers beautified the therapeutic work and made of it a religion in the spirit of the original gospel. Such consecration borders too nearly on the greatest self-sacrifice to attract many of us. Consequently there still remain to be accomplished those greater works which were said of old to be made possible only by "fasting and prayer."

It would doubtless open a new field of thought for some if they should try out the idea of spiritual influx, that is, by putting emphasis on the incoming *life* as the decisive element rather than upon the thought which may be only an effect of this life. For this conception of our spiritual nature involves emphasis on the will or love as prior to and more interior than the understanding. More explicitly, the Divine love is said to flow into the will and the Divine wisdom to flow into the understanding or intellect. The "inmost" region of the spirit first receives the influx before it enters what we commonly know as the "mind." If we then think of the understanding as receiving this life after it has touched "the heart" as love, and distributing it through the inner world in general, we have a way of thinking about the operation of the healing power which produces the decisive nervous change and touches the bodily organism. The ideal then is that we may be so open at the centre that the Divine life shall freely course through our affections, quicken our thoughts, and pass without let or hindrance into our activities as a whole. Perfect spiritual health would be the result.

Reverend Mr. Evans incorporated this idea of the Divine influx into his interpretation of the Quimby philosophy before publishing his first book, "The Mental Cure," 1869. But very little has been made of this view. The result of its adoption would be a more thorough study of the whole relationship of the soul to the body. It would then be important to distinguish between the two influxes, that from the spiritual world and that from the natural. If we understood the latter influx better we might in time have an adequate idea of our heredity, and we should see why the new therapy has sometimes failed.

Our interest in the elaborate process should not however keep us from concentrating upon the working ideas which bring direct results. Granted that the quickening impetus comes from the Divine love, and that love or sympathy on our part is the central motive, we naturally seek the most practical means of realizing it in actual service. And so the question arises whether in giving silent treatment one should think of the specific trouble or need on the part of the patient.

This depends upon the case. Sometimes a general realization is effective without direct thought of the patient or his needs. The healer's spirit, absorbed in contemplation of the "perfect love" which casts out fear, the peace "which passeth all understanding," may be instrumental in the best sense of the word in overcoming the nervousness, excitement, or irritability in the patient. But there are cases which are reached only through detailed understanding, followed by specific realization. Patients differ in temperament, also. Some readily respond to a general realization, while others are unyielding in type. The intuitive healer believes there is guidance for every occasion and every case. He does not assume to control the whole situation. He seeks to do what is given him to do, in the Divine wisdom.

Should we treat the subjective mind?

This term, "subjective mind," suggests Hudson's, "The Law of Psychic Phenomena," with its artificial distinction between the subjective and the objective. Actual mental life does not appear to confirm the distinction. Those who ask this question are apt to believe that the whole trouble with us is subjective, that is, there is something hidden which can be taken from us as a tooth might be extracted, leaving us free to go on thinking and living as before. It would then be a question of finding the right combination in each case, the suggestion which strikes home. But not even a prejudice comes forth thus easily. We are on the road to freedom from a prejudice when we catch ourselves in the act of expressing it, when we note that it *is* a prejudice and undesirable, and will to overcome it. Nothing can take the place of recognition. And recognition is conscious, not "subjective." Spiritual healing is not a process to be performed on us only while we sleep. Our woes have sprung in part from our own conduct. We have been sowing as well as reaping. Our responsibility still remains, even when it is partly a question of unconscious complexes which must be brought to the surface.

There are indeed inner and outer phases of *the same mind.* There is a difference between inner thought, thought "with the spirit," and thought as most people know it when they use their brains in intellectual work. There is intuition. There is guidance. We come to know what spiritual thinking is by learning about the secret place. What we need is more intimate knowledge of the spirit in contrast with bodily life. What should be treated is the whole self. And silent treatment is a means to an end, the end being the inculcation of that spiritual wisdom which shows people how to live. Some of the former therapeutists gave up the practice of treating silently many years ago, in favor of the more important work of helping people to understand themselves as spiritual beings. The so-called "subjective" is only a small part of this our total spiritual selfhood.

What is the function of the subconscious mind in healing?

Again, the question suggests theories involving exaggerated emphasis, to the neglect of our conscious selfhood. What is needed is a clear conception of the unconscious, the subconscious and the conscious in proper relation.

Most of the mental elements of disease are in the realm of the unconscious, so far as the patient is concerned, although all these are related to the life he leads, that is, to conduct. Consequently the hidden causes need to be brought to light, the repressed desires, the dissatisfactions, the inner conflicts, the gnawing fears, the suppressed emotional complexes, or what not. The healer discerns and understands these first. He then explains them to the patient in the re-educational work following upon the treatment. The patient then has opportunity to change his attitude, if he will; to lead a wiser life, with less friction, decreasing fear, less worry, less rebellion and conflict. If the patient thus wills to modify his life in accordance with the new possibilities put before him, beneficial subconscious after-effects will follow. But nothing can take the place of coming to judgment. The subconscious mind is not a miracle-worker. It must be given its cue. It is as obedient as a shadow. It is a phase of consciousness in general, not a separate "mind."

How is absent healing possible?

In the same way as a silent treatment given when the patient is present. There is as much to explain in the case of healing which takes place when the patient is three feet away as when he is six hundred miles distant. Silent treatment, that is, healing without manipulation or the use of electricity, medicine, hypnotic "passes," or any other visible device, takes place through inner affinity, "vibration," telepathy or some mode of communication which we may briefly call "wireless." The explanation usually offered is that it occurs through the operation of faculties or senses higher than those functioning through the brain. These powers are said to act independently of space. Hence space is no obstacle—unless *the idea* of space stands in our way.

Whether it is desirable to try to heal people absently whom we have never seen is a different matter. Those who are conscientious will ordinarily say that they must first know the patient, for they need some clue or means of identification. A highly intuitive healer might discern this clue at a distance.

Why do former patients sometimes relapse into their old troubles?

Because there has been no real interior change. There may have been a glossing over through acceptance of some form of mental therapy involving denials rather than understanding. This may have given the appearance of a cure. The illusion may have been kept up for years. But nature always compels us to disclose our hidden illusions after a while.

Our deeper troubles are apt to be temperamental. We may find some temporary remedy in the form of a theory that is pleasing. But eventually we need to see just how our temperamental tendencies cause our trouble; for example, in the case of a highly emotional or artistic temperament, an impulsive or high-strung type. Hence life brings us to the point where we must face the underlying attitude or prevailing love which has entered into all that has brought us our trouble.

What is the connection between healing and psychical experiences?

It would take a whole volume to answer this question adequately. In "The Open Vision" I have argued that in this new age we are working forward into insight where all seemed dark, because of ignorance of the powers that function in us when we are psychically active, and because we have failed to discriminate between experiences which can be explained from within the personality and those which may be said to imply the presence of angels or spirits. The "open vision" of old was possible when there was spiritual perception and innocence, in the world's spiritual childhood. People came to believe in spiritual realities because they enjoyed spiritual experiences. Later generations believed in such realities because of doctrines referring to such experiences, when "there was no longer any open vision." We in our day are passing beyond the doctrinal stage to the period of verification through inner experience. We need to know spiritual experience as such before we can understand "psychical" experiences. For we need vision, a standard, wisdom. Hence it is important for us to grow in spiritual understanding rather than in the cultivation of anything bordering on the psychic.

Now, in spiritual healing we, of course, use the same powers, such as intuition, clairvoyance, clairaudience, the discernment of "mental atmospheres" at a distance, talking "with the spirit," as in experiences set apart from another point of view as "psychical." But we ordinarily call them "spiritual," because we seek to realize the Eternal Presence, not to commune with "spirits." Hence there is a difference of motive or interest. Spiritual healing may be practised without concerning oneself with psychical phenomena, popularly so-called. It is better thus. Then one may come to see that such a work pursued through the years has brought the mind into possession of a standard by which to judge the psychical.

Again, it is important to help the sick to see their way through to spiritual understanding. Psychism is a kind of disease, with some. There is need of spiritual re-education and enlightenment. It is not orderly to seek communications with departed spirits.

As indicated in "The Open Vision," Dr. Quimby acquired the same powers in high degree which people with spiritistic interests would have cultivated so as to become psychics. But he steered clear of the psychical side-issues and used his clairvoyance and his other powers in the spiritual diagnosis of disease and the alleviation of human suffering. In his writings, as recently published in "The Quimby Manuscripts," we find one of his strong reasons. Spiritualism was just then coming into extensive vogue. Mediums claimed to summon up "the dead," and to heal by their aid. Dr. Quimby sought to make clear the way to spiritual healing through Divine aid, through *life* in contrast with the "the dead." The airy shapes summoned by mediums seemed to him creations of a person's belief. But what we need is something more than a product of our own fancy. We need that truth which will set men free.

Is it necessary to believe in obsession or demoniacal possession in order to explain certain types of obstinate disease or insanity?

This is a mooted question just now. We seem to be returning to a period when one can believe anything once classified as superstition. In accordance with the principles advocated in the foregoing chapters, let us say that our direct concern in any case is with the centre of attraction and development which has brought the given individual where he is today. Let us then look as deeply as we can, and ever more deeply into his inner life to discover its hidden complexes and its points of contact. Even if we believe in obsession we would need to break the connection from within. We are primarily concerned with these inner connections. We may well undertake to explain as many of them as possible in terms of what has been going on within the self, with its instincts and impulses, its habits and emotions, its desires and inner conflicts. Whatever may be outside the self, it is to the self just what it appears to be in terms of what the self believes. Thus a temptation may be objectified into a contest with the Devil. But our devils subside out of the objective as we grow in wisdom and in psychology. At last we come face to face with self-love, and that is demon enough.

What light does Mr. Myers's theory of the subliminal self throw on spiritual healing?

A very clear light. In terms of this theory, most of the self lies below the level or threshold of consciousness, as we ordinarily know it; the deeper or "subliminal" self has wider points of contact with reality, including realities in the spiritual world. Thus the mathematical prodigy is able to give immediate answer to a complex problem ordinarily involving long processes of computation. Thus genius in general is explicable. So, too, P. P. Quimby had wider contacts of a certain type enabling him to have direct communion with the energy or power through which he accomplished his works of healing. Essential to this deeper process was his clairvoyance or intuition, which disclosed the states to be healed in patients of many types.

According to this theory we come nearer understanding what the spirit is and what it can accomplish. We see that it undoubtedly possesses what Quimby called "spiritual senses," as counterparts of the natural senses. That is, we possess not only clairvoyance ("telesthesia" or inner vision) and clairaudience (inner audition), but other direct perceptions which include the discernment of "mental atmospheres," the detection of what Quimby called "odors," perceptible at a distance. There are "emergences" or "uprushes" from the subliminal which disclose processes that have been going on subconsciously. There is a sense of independence of space. Then too in some cases there may be what Myers calls a "clairvoyant excursion" by which information is gained at a distance as if by self-projection.

All these abilities appear to be needed in order to explain actual experiences.

The explanation is safer in Myers's hands, because he keeps close to the facts of psychical research and does not allow himself to adopt the extravagances of popular believers in the "subconscious mind." One may find in this clear-cut theory of the subliminal self a way to develop a sound spiritual psychology. We may then see how it was possible for Quimby to discern what we call the unconscious portion of a patient's life, long before the days of psycho-analysis and the Freudian technique. A spiritual discernment which should be as far-reaching as his would disclose more elements in the hidden life than any mere psycho-analysis of dreams or suppressed complexes. The study of the implied points of contact below the threshold of consciousness would take us into the wide region of relationship or correspondence with the spiritual world. Myers sought an explanation of the whole human self in relation to that world and the natural world as well. His insight opened up the most promising vistas for our study. And we need scope. A specialist's theory, like that of Freud with his analysis of dreams, is likely to leave us in a limited region, with exaggerated emphasis on one or more of the instincts. Again, we are apt to be limited by the physiological psychology of the day, as if the whole sphere of the unconscious and the subconscious could be reduced to states of the brain. In contrast with these special views, Myers's interpretation of the subliminal self opens up the whole field of the relationship between the present world of experience and the future life.

The various inquiries tend however to converge. We need not be negative or sceptical in our attitude toward the "subconscious mind" just because over-emphasis has been put upon it. The tendency of thought in this field is toward the conviction that there are deeper or more interior receptivities, wider or more varied points of contact in the subliminal than as conscious beings we are aware of. This is a great truth. Then with this truth let us not fail to put that no less important one, namely, that however great the powers of our hidden nature nothing ever takes the place of consciousness as selective and volitional. In the long run everything goes back to what we love most as conscious beings. If there is an open door in our consciousness with regard to spiritual realities there will be an open door subconsciously. But if our hearts are closed up here on the level of consciousness, we in vain expect our subconscious mind to be open-hearted. Consciousness was given us for judgment, for choice, for moral decision. Granted a volition in favor of love to God and man, the rest of our nature will do its best to carry it out into the realm of conduct. What we love most affects the whole self, however we may name its various departments. What we love most affects the whole realm of our conduct too. So any special interest, such as spiritual healing, is concerned with the prevailing love. And the more directly we can appeal to the love-nature to change from selfishness in any of its forms to service and love to God, the more will all the other special interests having to do with the human self be benefited also.

THE END.